D0277074

meditations
for your
pregnancy

meditations
for your
pregnancy

Sheila Lavery & Pippa Duncan

CARROLL & BROWN PUBLISHERS LIMITED

To Cameron PIPPA DUNCAN
For my mother SHEILA LAVERY

First published in 2000 in the
United Kingdom by:

CARROLL & BROWN PUBLISHERS LIMITED
20 LONSDALE ROAD
QUEEN'S PARK
LONDON NW6 6RD

SENIOR MANAGING EDITOR RACHEL ARIS

MANAGING ART EDITOR ADELLE MORRIS
DESIGNERS RACHEL GOLDSMITH, EVIE LOIZIDES

PHOTOGRAPHER JULES SELMES

Copyright © 2000 Carroll & Brown Limited

Text copyright © 2000 Sheila Lavery and Pippa Duncan

A CIP catalogue record for this book is available from the British Library.

ISBN 1-903258-04-9

Reproduced by Master Image Pte Ltd, Singapore

Printed and bound in Italy by LEGO

First edition

The moral right of Sheila Lavery and Pippa Duncan to be identified as the authors of this work has been asserted in accordance with the Copyright, Designs and Patents Act of 1988.

All rights reserved. No part of this publication may be reproduced in any material form (including photocopying or storing it in any medium by electronic means and whether or not transiently or incidentally to some other use of this publication) without the written permission of the copyright owner, except in accordance with the provisions of the Copyright, Designs and Patents Act of 1988 or under the terms of a licence issued by the Copyright Licensing Agency, 90 Tottenham Court Road, London W1P 9HE. Applications for the copyright owner's written permission to reproduce any part of this publication should be addressed to the publisher.

Contents

Why meditate during pregnancy?

If you're planning a pregnancy, or you're pregnant already, you're embarking on one of the most creative, most inspiring experiences of your life. It is also one of the most challenging. One day you'll be a picture of health, full of excitement and energy, the next you'll feel nauseous and tired and find yourself overcome by inexplicable weepiness.

To make the most of your pregnancy, you need to learn to listen to your body, to respect your feelings, to nap when you need to (without feeling guilty) or to tear around organising the baby's room if the urge overtakes you. Meditating can help you achieve all this by enabling you to relax and focus on what's important, thereby ensuring that the conception, pregnancy and birth of your child are as wonderful as possible.

You may have certain preconceptions about meditation, but it isn't strange or difficult: it is a simple and enriching natural state of relaxed concentration within the easy grasp of absolutely anyone. It helps keep your body healthy and puts worries into perspective, so you can provide the most natural and nurturing environment a baby could want.

This book includes a whole variety of meditation techniques designed specially for use when you are trying to conceive, at each stage of pregnancy, and following delivery. They are gleaned from many different sources, ranging from ancient traditions to the most up-to-date practices in obstetrics and antenatal care. The aim is to give you a choice of relaxation techniques that not only have a practical purpose for your pregnancy but can also be spiritually and emotionally uplifting. Some exercises take time, privacy and a little practice. Others are much shorter, and can be performed anywhere – on your way to work, in the doctor's crowded waiting room, when you're preparing dinner; these are intended to keep you relaxed and calm throughout the day.

The twentieth-century mystic, Osho, once said: 'Meditation is nothing but coming back home, just to have a little rest inside.' We hope that our book will inspire and assist you to meditate regularly before, during and after your pregnancy, enabling you to achieve that feeling of coming home and find within yourself a little place to rest each day.

What is meditation?

Meditation is the collective term for a number of techniques used to calm and re-energise the mind and body using the powers of concentration. It is commonly referred to as a state of 'relaxed awareness'. This is because meditation is unlike sleep or any other form of relaxation in that it relaxes the body while retaining a high level of mental alertness. During meditation, the constant chatter of our thoughts is stilled to bring about a state of tranquillity and profound rest that can eliminate tension, benefit you and your baby, and generally enhance your quality of life.

People meditate for a whole variety of reasons, including relaxation, improved mental and physical health, peace of mind, enhanced concentration, creativity and self-knowledge. Meditation can also serve a spiritual purpose. Mystics and spiritual leaders believe that it is the path that leads to God or enlightenment. All the great religions of the world have at some time emphasised the importance of meditation as a spiritual tool, but it is the Buddhist and Hindu traditions with which it is most closely identified.

The physical benefits of meditation depend largely on the fact that it evokes in the body what is known as the 'relaxation response' (a term coined by Dr Herbert Benson, Associate Professor at Harvard Medical School and President of the Mind/Body Medical Institute; *see also page 13*), which helps alleviate the harmful effects of stress. Temporary stress can be a positive influence in life: it enables us to deal effectively with challenging situations, when we need to make difficult decisions, for instance, or we want to fuel the creative spark. But many of us live with prolonged or excessive levels of stress, meaning our bodies are never given the opportunity to relax.

The traditional lotus position or half-lotus shown here is common in Eastern statues of Buddhas or yogis, but can be difficult for Westerners to achieve.

Why do we need to relax?

Chronic stress is detrimental to health. In fact, some doctors believe that up to 90 percent of ill health can be attributed to stress. This is due in part to the physiological changes that occur during the so-called 'fight or flight' or stress response – the body's physical reaction to a perceived threat of any kind. During the fight or flight response, hormones are released from the adrenal glands to make the heart beat faster. Breathing becomes more rapid and blood is diverted away from the non-essential organs (such as the digestive system) and to the muscles in the limbs, priming the body either to stay and fight or to beat a hasty retreat. Once the danger has passed, the body reverts to its natural, balanced state.

While this is an apt reaction to physical peril, in today's world stress is more likely to come in the form of emotional demands or anxiety, to which such a physical response is inappropriate. Yet the body makes no distinction in its response to stress signals. At the end of a hard day at work, the body will have been constantly tensed for action, with stress hormones building up all day, but the tension is never released and the body is given no chance to normalise. This is what has such a negative effect on our health, resulting in hypertension (high blood pressure, also common in pregnancy), stomach ulcers, mental exhaustion, muscle pain, a lowering of the body's immune system and many other complaints.

> *Meditate in the morning and evening and at night before you go to bed. Sit quietly for about two minutes. You will find everything in your life falling into place and your prayers answered.*
>
> YOGA SWAMI, POSITIVE THOUGHTS FOR DAILY MEDITATIONS

What happens during meditation?

Meditation is one of the most effective ways to bring about a state of profound rest in mind and body, not only helping us cope with stress itself, but also reversing the effects of the fight or flight response. Readings from electroencephalographs (EEGs) – instruments that measure electrical impulses in the brain – show that during meditation the left hemisphere of the brain (associated with logical, verbal, linear and time-linked thinking) becomes less active, while the right hemisphere (associated with intuition and holistic, creative thinking) becomes more active. This shift appears to reduce the verbal demands being processed by the brain, demands placed on us by others as well as those we place on ourselves. The result is that the meditator 'switches off' the normal thought process, becomes less self-critical and enjoys a guilt-free rest.

The brain waves associated with meditation are those of both sleep and wakefulness. While the mind remains fully aware, clear, sharp and focused, the body enjoys deep relaxation similar to that of the deepest sleep. As a natural response to changes in brain wave activity, body functioning also starts to change. The sympathetic nervous system (which registers the body's stress response) is switched off and the parasympathetic nervous system (which promotes rest and relaxation) is switched on. This complex nerve network is linked to every organ and body function, so when it rests the entire body gets a chance to normalise. Metabolism and breathing slow down; blood does not need to be pumped around the body so quickly, slowing the heart rate and reducing blood pressure; the functioning of the digestive system returns to normal as blood flows away from the relaxed limb muscles; cholesterol and stress hormone levels decrease; and immune function improves. Anxiety levels also drop significantly. This sort of deep relaxation creates the perfect state for healing, recuperation and repair.

MEDITATION MYTHS

✦ Meditation is not a means of escape from the outside world. We meditate in order to function more effectively in the world, not run away from it.

✦ It is neither falling asleep nor going into a trance.

✦ It is not cultish or unnatural.

✦ It is not just sitting quietly for ten minutes: it requires conscious effort to remain calm yet vigilant.

✦ It is not being selfish. Time spent meditating is an investment in your health and happiness.

✦ Meditation is not a substitute for medical care.

Meditating during the pregnancy year

Anyone with a busy life will gain from regular meditation, but pregnant women in particular will notice its benefits as their body, emotions and lifestyle change in preparation for motherhood.

Physical benefits

The relaxation response induced by meditation creates a natural state of internal harmony that provides the best environment for a growing baby and the healthiest condition for a pregnant woman. The benefits start even before pregnancy begins – meditation can help to overcome problems with conception.

Stress is strongly implicated as a cause of infertility in both men and women. It appears to reduce the levels of reproductive hormones, while the cortical steroids have been shown to act like an inbuilt contraceptive, excessive amounts inhibiting ovulation in women and sperm production in men. By reducing stress and minimising its impact on body chemistry, meditation can help to combat stress-related infertility.

Research has shown that meditating can also help to reduce or eliminate any dependence on cigarettes, drugs and alcohol, all of which are detrimental to your fertility and a baby's development. Equally important, especially during pregnancy, is its ability to lower blood pressure, reduce muscle pain and sickness, improve sleep quality and boost energy levels.

Psychological benefits

People who meditate regularly tend to agree that it makes them more creative, energetic and productive. Meditation increases your powers of concentration and the ability to screen out unimportant or obstructive thoughts and emotions. This can help you access resources you never knew you had, increase your self-worth and sense of identity, and help you feel more in control of your problems. This mental focus is particularly helpful for mothers-to-be as it will reduce the anxiety common during pregnancy and plays a valuable role in overcoming postpartum depression.

Reduces stress, promotes relaxation, enhances creativity, improves sleep

Improves breathing, can help to combat breathlessness, which is most common at 16–20 weeks, and helps during labour

Lowers blood pressure and reduces the risk of pre-eclampsia

Increases blood circulation to digestive system, helps combat morning sickness and constipation

Relaxes your baby

Reduces muscle tension and backache

Perhaps more than anything, meditation instils a deep sense of peace that radiates out to all areas of life. It brings clarity and order to psychological health and is spiritually uplifting. Meditators tend to be less aggressive, and more loving and willing to reconcile disputes, which is of huge bene-fit when a relationship is going through the changes that impending parenthood can bring (see Meditating with a partner, *pages 34–35*). The calm process of reflection that characterises meditation also encourages a deep communication and bonding with your baby at every stage of your pregnancy.

What does it feel like to meditate?

Meditation is often referred to as an 'altered state of consciousness' and this can lead many people to think they will feel strange when meditating. In fact, it is a completely natural feeling that many people experience during the day without realising. When you are relaxed, quiet and completely absorbed in looking, thinking, or doing one thing (reading a book, for example) you can experience the meditative state of mind.

When you start a meditation, the most overwhelming feeling is likely to be one of relaxation, a drifting sensation similar to the feeling you experience just before falling asleep. You may even drop off! With practice, however, you will be able to relax but remain mentally alert. Unwanted thoughts or emotions sometimes sur-face during a meditation – part of the art of meditating is learning to let these thoughts drift by as if they were clouds floating across the sky. Do not try to stop them or follow them, simply let them come and go. Your body may feel heavy as it begins to wind down, and then feel light and floating. Your breathing will slow down, possibly with pauses between breaths; and as blood is rerouted from the limb muscles to the skin as you relax, you may notice a tingling sensation in the skin.

Learning to meditate

There are many ways to meditate and the most popular techniques are described opposite. All share a similar goal: to induce a state of deep, ben-eficial rest in the whole person. No single method suits everyone, so try several and you are bound to find one (or a combination) that suits your preferences. The meditation exercises in this book adopt many different approaches to offer as wide a variety of techniques as possible.

THE MANY FACES OF MEDITATION

✦ Transcendental meditation (TM)

Possibly the best known form of meditation, TM was brought to the West in the late 1950s by an Indian holy man, Maharishi Mahesh Yogi. Devised for easy practice in the busy, modern world, it is distinguished from other forms of meditation by the use of a personalised mantra (a short phrase), on which you effortlessly allow your attention to rest, so that other thoughts become insignificant. TM can be learned only from a teacher, who chooses the mantra for each student; students are obliged to keep their mantras secret. Unlike other mantra-based meditations, TM uses mantras with no meaning: actual words are considered too distracting as they may relate to significant images or memories. Much of the medical research into the benefits of meditation has been carried out in relation to TM, possibly because TM is taught in a standardised way, making it easier to assess scientifically.

✦ Buddhist meditation

Many meditation techniques are based on simple Buddhist practices, and in particular 'the Mindfulness of Breathing' and the *Metta Bhavana* ('the Development of Loving Kindness'). The first technique involves concentrating on and counting breaths to clear the mind of all thoughts. You then use the *Metta Bhavana* to focus on a happy moment in your life, bringing that happiness into the present and extending it to yourself and others. In a twenty-minute meditation, you would perhaps spend five minutes each focusing the happiness on yourself, on a friend, on someone to whom you are indifferent and on someone you dislike or has annoyed you. You could also do this by repeating a specific phrase such as, 'May I be well, may you be well' Buddhist meditation may also involve using a small object such as a flower, shell or candle as a focus.

✦ Clinically standardised meditation (CSM)

This is the most modern form of meditation available and is based on traditional meditation methods, but stripped of spiritual associations. Devised by clinical psychologist, Dr Patricia Carrington, it was developed to be so simple it could be used by anyone. As in traditional techniques, the breath, a mentally repeated sound, word or another simple focal point is used, but the repetition of a sound is used almost effortlessly, without being paced or intentionally linked to the breathing pattern. The method is flexible, designed to fit in with individual needs and lifestyles, so you can do it at any time – sitting, lying down or even commuting to work. Meditation time is also flexible, usually between ten and forty minutes a day.

✦ The respiratory one method

Developed by Dr Herbert Benson, this is primarily a medical technique, like CSM. However, practising it takes a little more mental discipline. You sit comfortably, relax, focus on your breathing and mentally repeat the word 'one' every time you breathe out. The focus is therefore the breath and the word 'one', which are linked together.

> *It is the experience of meditation that brings about therapeutic change, rather than the techniques used to evoke this experience.*
>
> DR PATRICIA CARRINGTON

Making meditation your own

While some people follow a particular meditation technique, others find it more beneficial to tailor techniques to meet their own needs. You can devise your own technique as long as you bear in mind that certain elements are essential to all successful meditation. These include: making time to meditate every day; choosing the right environment and the most comfortable position (these can change from day to day, depending on the purpose of the meditation and the stage of your pregnancy); having a winding-down procedure to free your muscles from tension; focusing on a single word, phrase, or object to still your mind; and disregarding without effort all intrusive thoughts. These are the elements which form the basis of all the exercises in this book, and are explored in more detail on the following pages.

The secrets of success

Making the commitment to learn meditation is the first and most important step towards effective practice. However, even the keenest students can get impatient or become disheartened in the early stages. To increase your chances of successfully mastering the art of meditation, bear in mind the following points:

- *Believe you can do it. You need no special talents. Everyone can meditate, although it may come more easily to some than to others.*
- *Be disciplined and dedicated. This is what separates the successes from the failures. The techniques may be simple but the human mind is not; it takes patience and practice to focus on one thought, word or image for even a minute without giving in to distraction.*
- *When you find a method that works, stick to it.*
- *Try to find a special place in your home or garden where you would like to meditate and use that as your sanctuary.*
- *Practise regularly. Meditation is not like taking an aspirin for a headache; try to make it part of your routine. If you can, practise twice daily at the same time each day.*
- *Start by meditating for five minutes and gradually increase the time to twenty minutes. If you want to time yourself, use a kitchen timer that is not too loud; otherwise just come out of the meditation when you feel ready. You'll soon get a good idea of time.*

How
to meditate

Although Buddhist monks devote years to perfecting their meditations, recent research has shown that simple techniques practised daily can have significant benefits within weeks. This is because meditation is a journey rather than a destination. Everyone's journey is unique: it progresses at different rates, every stage has something to offer, and there is no 'right' way to travel. Because no one technique works for everyone, you need to consider several factors to decide what will be best for you.

The first is to find a focus. There are many to choose from, such as counting your breaths or using a mantra. The rule of thumb here is to choose the one to which you are instinctively drawn. If that doesn't work, try another. Sometimes people start with what they believe to be the easiest technique, usually breath counting, but later find they can meditate more effectively using a mantra or a visualisation. The surest way to test the efficacy of any method is to ask yourself if you feel better after the meditation than you did before. If you do, then it is working for you. It is best to avoid flitting between several techniques, so stick with the most successful, practise it daily, and substitute it for any of the techniques mentioned in the exercises.

While learning to meditate, it helps to prepare your body and mind. Try to meditate when you are feeling alert and rested, and if possible avoid alcohol for at least a day beforehand. You should also abstain from smoking, eating or drinking caffeinated drinks for an hour beforehand as these can all interfere with your mood. And make your surroundings are as conducive as possible.

Later you will find that you carry meditation with you wherever you go; whenever your attention is totally absorbed in one activity, thought or image, you are in a state of meditation. This means that you can bring meditation into your everyday activities as well as practising it in isolation. Throughout this book we have included simple, quick exercises that will help you meditate on the move, when twenty minutes alone is out of the question. All of the information is aimed at making meditation as easy as possible, but only you can make it real. So, do what works for you and don't give up!

Essential elements

All meditation techniques have certain elements in common. In theory these can be narrowed down to two basic steps: focusing on a single word, phrase, sound, object or your breath; and passively disregarding all other intrusive thoughts or distractions. But in practice most meditation teachers agree that learning to meditate is easier if you follow certain guidelines. The information on the following pages is aimed at helping you learn to meditate effectively. It may be necessary only to observe certain elements, such as sitting comfortably, for a short while: when you have learned to meditate sitting with your eyes closed in a quiet room, you can gradually become more flexible in your practice, meditating with your eyes open, while standing or walking, in any posture or situation, even in the labour ward!

Finding time

Some people are reluctant to learn how to meditate because they worry it will be too time-consuming. But it really needn't eat up too much of your day. Try to think of your meditation time as an investment. By taking a few minutes out of your day you can become more productive and energetic so you can use the rest of your time more effectively. Regular meditators also tend to need less sleep, so after a short time you may find that you get up earlier and stay active for longer.

Research has proved that meditating twice a day for fifteen to twenty minutes is the most effective way to reap the rewards. But it is more important to make the effort to meditate for some time every day than to become obsessed with time-keeping.

What time is best?

In India it is traditional to meditate between 3 and 4 o'clock in the morning as this is the *Brahma Muhurta*, the Hour of God. People who follow this practice believe that this time is so conducive to meditation that it enables even complete beginners to meditate effectively. However, this is not an option for most people (particularly for pregnant women!) and a better alternative may be first thing in the morning, before you get involved in your day's activities, and last thing at night, before bedtime. Whatever time you choose, try to establish a pattern by meditating at the same time every day: if you miss your usual slot it is often difficult to find another during the day.

When you're deciding on a suitable time to meditate that fits in with your lifestyle, it might help to consider the following:

- *Which times of the day are least demanding for you?*
- *When are you most likely to be alone and undisturbed?*
- *When could you introduce a break into your day, every day?*
- *If you have a busy schedule, could you get up ten minutes earlier in the morning?*

Relaxation

This is the starting point of any meditation. Conscious relaxation relieves anxiety, which tends to 'scatter' your thoughts, and releases physical tension, which can be distracting if it causes discomfort or pain. Being able to relax at will and in any situation is not only invaluable during pregnancy, it will also help you meet the challenge of labour as relaxation interrupts the cycle of fear, tension and pain and allows you to enjoy the birth. When you learn how to relax voluntarily you will soon be able to relax quickly, in any position and in any situation.

Simple relaxation

The easiest way to learn how to relax is to find a quiet place where you will not be disturbed. Unplug the phone, make sure you are warm enough and sit or lie comfortably with your eyes closed. Let your breathing become slow and gentle, and as you breathe out, sigh to release the tension in your body. You can also relieve specific areas of tension by focusing on each part of your body, tightening it and then letting go. For example, think about your shoulders, push them down and notice where you hold your tension. Breathe out and, as you do, release your shoulders. Beginning either at your head or your toes, work though each body part in this way. When you first start to practise relaxation, you may feel sleepy as your adrenaline levels drop. Try to avoid sleep by keeping your mind focused, while allowing your body to be free from tension.

While practising a relaxation technique, notice how it feels to be relaxed. Observe how your breathing changes, and concentrate on any sensations you were unaware of before. You may feel light and loose, or soft and heavy. Your skin may feel warm and tingly, your stomach may gurgle and you may see colours before your eyes or have a sensation of floating. Everyone feels something different when they relax, but it always feels good. If you're pregnant, you may find that your baby becomes more active as you become relaxed. This shows how sensitive your unborn baby is and how quickly he or she responds to changes occurring within you. Remember that your baby also benefits from your periods of relaxation.

On-the-spot relaxation

When relaxing in a quiet room is not an option, you can adapt the above technique to use in an instant. Think 'relax', push your shoulders down, and as you breathe out with a long sigh, let all the tension from your head to your toes flow out with it. Another simple technique is to take three deep breaths, and with each slow exhalation feel the tension flow out on your breath as your shoulders sag and your belly softens.

What position is best for meditating?

Your mind cannot become still if you are constantly shifting, fidgeting and trying to get comfortable, so it is important to think about your posture when you meditate. This doesn't mean you have to twist yourself into the lotus position to meditate effectively! Forcing your body into a difficult position that that you are not used to could do you physical damage and cause so much discomfort it becomes impossible to meditate. Find a position you can hold without becoming restless, and that will stop you from slumping or being too rigid. Each of the postures discussed opposite has a different mental and emotional effect – listen to your body and be guided by its changing needs, bearing in mind the following considerations:

- *Make yourself comfortable, but not so comfortable that you fall asleep.*
- *Sit in a relaxed upright position, not slumped or rigid, but so that your spine is straight and your breath can move freely.*
- *Aim for balance and 'openness' in your posture. Do not cross your arms or your legs, if sitting on a chair. Unclench your fists and rest a hand on each leg, preferably with palms facing upwards.*
- *Choose a posture that you can hold for ten to twenty minutes.*

Try to sit in a special place that you can associate with meditation. Keep it clear of clutter and introduce a vase of flowers or a special picture. You could also use an essential oil vaporizer to scent the air with an aroma such as frankincense, which slows and deepens the breath and is conducive to meditation.

FINDING A SUITABLE POSITION

The following positions are suitable for any stage of pregnancy, but experiment until you find one that works for you.

✦ Lotus position

It is traditional but by no means essential to sit in the lotus position, which symbolises balance and provides the body with a firm base. A few Westerners find this position easy to maintain and feel it encourages a state of relaxed awareness and mental clarity, but others find it impossible to master. The half lotus, shown here, may be easier to hold during late pregnancy.

✦ Supported by a cushion

Sit cross-legged on a large, firm cushion tilted slightly forwards, stopping you from slumping in the small of your back. Various wedges, benches and special meditation cushions are available, but a cushion or pillows is perfectly adequate. Don't fold your arms across your body, but sit with your back erect and your shoulders back, opening up your chest cavity so you can breathe freely.

✦ In an upright chair

If you prefer not to sit on the floor, you can meditate sitting in a straight-backed chair. Resist the temptation to sink into the nearest couch or armchair, as this will allow you to slouch and make you feel drowsy. Sit with your feet flat on the floor, about a shoulder's width apart, and use a cushion or pillow to support your lower back. Rest your hands in your lap or on your knees. If, as your abdomen becomes larger, you find this position a bit cramped, try sitting closer to the edge of the chair and spread your feet a little further apart.

✦ Lying down

The 'corpse pose' is great if you find it hard to relax. But beware: it is very easy to fall asleep in this position! Lie on your back, preferably with a mattress or folded blanket beneath you and allow the tension to flow out of your limbs by letting them flop gently. As your pregnancy progresses, you may prefer to lie with a pillow beneath your head and your feet and lower legs propped up on a chair, or alternatively on your side. Eventually you should be able to meditate in any position – sitting, standing, walking or lying down.

Concentration

Meditation occurs as the result of concentration on a single thought, word, image or activity. By focusing only on a single point in the present, you withdraw from the senses, forget past or future and disregard all out-side activity. This sounds simple in theory, but it takes constant attention and vigilance to focus your mind for five, ten or twenty minutes. Few activities in everyday life demand constant attention to one point of focus for even seconds, never mind minutes. Usually, when we try to concen-trate, one thought leads to another and all sorts of feelings, emotions and associations crowd the mind. Without concentration, meditation is not possible, but it need not be so difficult to master. A whole variety of tech-niques will help you maintain your concentration, and these are described on the next few pages. When attempting to focus your mind, however, you may find the following points of help:

- *Choose a simple point of focus and devote your whole attention to it, for five minutes at first, gradually increasing to twenty minutes.*
- *Do not force your mind to concentrate. Keep it focused, but without effort. Simply decide that you will attend to one thing only and let it hold your attention, disregarding all distractions.*
- *When intrusive thoughts attempt to crowd in (and they will), don't try to push them away, just let them float by without giving them any importance.*
- *If your mind wanders, gently bring it back to your focus.*
- *Accept that you may not succeed at first – and keep trying!*

Unstructured meditation

If you find it difficult to concentrate, you could try a form of unstructured meditation. This allows you to think 'around' a word, image, idea or problem and simply focus on that. Choose an area of yourself or your life that you feel needs attention. Keep thinking about it, exploring both the facts about it and how you feel about it. For example, you could focus on loving your baby and ask yourself, 'If I was my baby how would I like to be carried/born/treated/loved...?' Or if you feel you are neglecting yourself you could ask, 'If I was the person I loved most in the world, how would I treat myself?' The idea is not to daydream or indulge in a free association of ideas, but to explore *only* the concept you have chosen. Meditate on your chosen subject for ten to fifteen minutes a day for a week and then increase the time to twenty to thirty for a second week. Many people find this is a wonderful way to resolve a particular problem.

Finding a focus

Meditation involves using a single focus to still the mind and create a state of inner tranquillity. Anything that absorbs your attention can act as a focus – an engrossing film, for example, can shut you off to everything apart from what is happening on screen. But in meditation it is common to focus on simple, natural phenomena, objects of beauty or something that has spiritual significance.

The breath

The simplest and often the best focus for meditation is your breathing. Most people who learn meditation begin with breath counting or breath awareness. It is taught so that you can practise doing only one easy thing at a time. Because you need no resources other than a relaxed awareness of your own breathing you can practise it anywhere, anytime and in any circumstances. The breath is rhythmical, balanced and natural, so

SIMPLE BREATH COUNTING

1 Sit in a comfortable position as described on pages 20–21.

2 Set a timer for fifteen minutes.

3 Relax and release inner tension by taking a deep breath and letting it out with a sigh.

4 Now begin to focus on each breath. Count your breaths up to five and then start again at one. You can either count 'one, two, three…' on each out-breath or you can count both the in- and out-breaths, for example 'one, one…two, two…three, three…'. Repeat until the fifteen minutes is up.

5 Let your body relax but keep your mind alert and focused on the counting. If you feel sleepy, straighten your posture.

6 When your time is up, open your eyes slowly, but do not get up for a minute. Notice if you feel different to how you did when you started the meditation.

observing it helps to relax the body and quiet the mind. All relaxation techniques and antenatal classes make use of breathing as a way of relieving tension and easing pain and anxiety.

If you choose the breath-counting technique described on page 23, try not to force or control your breath, just observe it as it comes and goes at its own pace, and feel how it moves and reverberates through your body. Relaxed breathing is not regular, so your counting should not be regular either. Try to match your counting to your natural breathing pattern rather than regulating your breath by the pace of your counting. Remember to relax and focus. If your mind wanders, gently steer it back. Do not be disappointed if you find it difficult to stay focused initially – just keep practising and you will improve.

Breath awareness techniques

If you prefer not to count, you can simply observe the movement of your breath in your body. Sitting relaxed, place one hand flat over your navel, the other just below your breasts. Breathe in and allow it to fill the lower part of your lungs, before moving down to your abdomen. If you are pregnant, let the air wash over your baby and expand your abdomen before moving back up to lift your ribs and spread out your collarbones. Allow the breath to flow through you, and follow it with your mind as it relaxes, clears and refreshes every part of your body with which it comes into contact. As you breathe out, do so slowly from the top downwards, deflating your ribs and then your belly as you exhale completely. Do this several times so that you become aware of what good breathing feels like.

Now close your eyes and continue to breathe as above, but do not follow it with your mind. Focus only on the movement of the breath in your abdomen – the way it rises and falls with every in- and out-breath. Keep breathing in this relaxed way with your concentration centred on your abdomen for fifteen minutes.

Alternatively, sit relaxed and upright, with your spine straight, your shoulders back and your hands resting on your knees. Close your eyes and focus in your mind's eye on the tip of your nose at the point where the air enters and leaves your body. In this meditation you inhale twice and exhale once: breathe in to fill your abdomen, feeling the breath push into your back and sides, hold, and then breathe in further to fill your chest and expand your rib cage; now pause; and then breathe out in one long, slow exhalation. Pause and repeat. Focus on the tip of your nose throughout.

Try to pay attention to your breath at other times of the day. Regular deep breathing that expands your lungs and abdomen will help to relax you and get you into the habit of breathing well.

Mantras

Many people find the best way to achieve mental stillness is through the repetition of a simple word, phrase or sound that is used to block the intrusion of other words and thoughts. The human mind can process hundreds of thoughts per second, but only one at a time. Thinking one thought repeatedly leaves no room for others to intrude, focuses the mind in one direction and frees it from the usual emotional congestion that typifies everyday thinking. The word or sound chosen for this purpose is known as a mantra, a Sanskrit term meaning 'instrument of thought'. In ancient Indian philosophy, a mantra was a sacred word or group of words repeated in prayer and incantation. Using a mantra in meditation is still considered by some to be more mystical or emotional than just focusing on the breath.

Silent or spoken mantras?

If you choose a word such as 'Relax' for your mantra, you can repeat the word mentally without having to say it aloud. But certain sounds are valued for their vibrational qualities, and you may want to say these aloud. The sound 'Om' is often described as the sound of creation. If you say this sound aloud and hold it, as in 'Ommmmmm', you can feel it vibrate on your lips and resonate through your body. This vibration in itself is believed to have a profound effect on mind and body.

Some people believe the words of a mantra should have a healing or mystical effect, for example, 'God is love', but a mantra can be a word or a sound without any real meaning. Often they are musical or rhythmic. All students of Transcendental Meditation have their own mantra, which they keep secret and use as a focus during each meditation. The word is harmless, often meaningless and has no psychological associations. Dr Herbert Benson, who devised the Respiratory One method (*see page 13*) suggests using simple secular words such as 'One' and 'Peace', or if you are religious a word or phrase from a prayer. Lawrence LeShan recommends in his now classic text, *How to Meditate*, a simple two-syllable sound such as 'Lah-dee'. To devise your own he suggests you open the telephone directory at random and use the first syllable of the first name you put your finger on, then repeat the process and link the two syllables to form a mantra. Ultimately, any word or sound that focuses the mind is a mantra.

Choosing a mantra

Simple, meaningless or inspiring words, short phrases or sounds work best as a mantra. You could try one of these – 'Peace', 'Love', 'Relax', 'One', 'Joy', 'All is one', 'We are one', 'Om', 'Om Ah', 'Shalom', 'Allah hu', 'God is love', 'Om mani padme hum' (Hail to the jewel in the lotus) – or use any other mantra of your own devising. However, some words should *not* be used as a mantra. The word 'Mother', for example, has too many psychological associations. Similarly, 'Birth' or 'Baby' are too emotional to still your mind.

Whichever mantra you choose, you can repeat it not just during a proper meditation but throughout the day, while doing the housework, going for a walk or waiting in the doctor's surgery. The simple repetition very quickly soothes and relaxes.

How to use your mantra

When you are sitting comfortably and relaxed, focus on your mantra and repeat it over and over again. You can say the mantra aloud or to yourself. Even if you choose to say it silently, it is sometimes a good idea to say it aloud to begin with and let it become progressively quieter until it becomes a whisper and then you internalise it completely. This way you can get a feel for it. Most people find it helpful to synchronise their mantra with their breathing, saying it on every out-breath, or on every in- and out-breath. You can also say your mantra independently of your breathing. Either way, focus on the word or sound to the exclusion of everything else. If your attention wanders, simply bring it back to your mantra. Saying it aloud can help to regain your attention.

Some people find mantras too boring to focus on for fifteen to twenty minutes. If using a mantra makes your mind drift rather than focus, return to simple breath counting or try one of the other techniques described on the following pages.

Affirmations

Affirmations are similar to mantras in that they are words or phrases that can be repeated over and over again throughout a meditation. But there are also some basic differences between the two. Affirmations are often phrases rather than single words. The words of an affirmation always have meaning and the meaning is more important than the sound. They also tend to be 'tagged on' to a meditation in which you use the breath as a focus rather than being the focus themselves.

A new branch of medicine called psycho-neuro-immunology or mind/body medicine is based on the belief that our thoughts, either positive or negative, have a physical impact on the body. For example, if you fear pain and discomfort then that is what you will feel. But if, on the contrary, you tell yourself you are healthy, relaxed and in control, then your body responds accordingly. Affirmations repeated frequently while you are in a relaxed state are readily accepted by the subconscious mind. The subconscious is much more powerful than conscious thought, and when it accepts an affirmation, it works relentlessly to make it a reality. Imagine the benefits such positive thinking could bring over the next few months when you feel tired, uncomfortable or anxious as you prepare for labour.

Here are some affirmations you might like to try:

* Today is a perfect day
* I am (we are) happy and well
* I am peaceful
* I love how relaxed and in control I feel
* I am complete
* My beautiful baby is wanted and welcomed
* I am loving and lovable
* I love and cherish my perfect baby
* I am willing to change and grow
* All is well

Guidelines for devising your own affirmations

The most effective affirmations are those that you devise yourself, as and when you need them. An affirmation can take any form you want, but if it is to be acceptable to the subconscious it has to be positive, in the present tense, and as powerful as possible. Use strong descriptive words such as 'vibrant', 'energetic', 'dynamic', 'wonderful' or 'lovable', and focus on what you want to create or achieve, *not* on what you want to avoid. For example, if you want to use an affirmation to help you overcome back pain do not say 'My back is pain free'. Instead try something like 'I can move with wonderful ease and freedom'.

Using an affirmation to prepare for meditation

You can use affirmations to confirm and encourage changes that are taking place in your body during the relaxation process. If you tell yourself in a calm and focused way to 'Slow down' or 'I am relaxed', your body tends to respond accordingly. As your body starts to relax, repeating an affirmation such as 'I feel warm and heavy' (if you do) can help you to become more aware of the physical sensations associated with relaxation, so it becomes easier for you to recognise when you are relaxed.

Using an affirmation when meditating

Sit down and make yourself comfortable in the usual way. Focus on your breathing or the movement of your breath in one part of your body. Keep focusing on your breath and when you feel relaxed, introduce your affirmation. Do not think about the affirmation, just repeat it silently and continuously to yourself, while remaining focused on your breath. You can repeat the affirmation in time with your breathing, but remember the breath, not the affirmation, is your focus. If you find it difficult to combine the two, let go of the affirmation until you feel more focused and return to it later. Combining your affirmation with a visualisation (*see pages 31–32*) can have even greater impact. If your affirmation is, 'My beautiful baby is healthy and well', hold an image in your mind of your perfect, healthy developing child.

Using affirmations in everyday life

You don't have to restrict affirmations to a formal meditation: you can use them whenever you need to give your mind positive instructions. For example, if you are anxiously awaiting the results of tests you could tell yourself, 'Everything is as it should be', or if you have been suffering from morning sickness you could begin your day with, 'This morning I feel happy and well'. In such situations, affirmations can have a positive effect on mind and body, but they do not produce the sort of relaxed awareness associated with meditation.

Using a visual aid

If you prefer to meditate with your eyes open, you can help to keep your mind focused by meditating on a pleasing image. The goal is to gaze at and be aware of the object, but not actively to think about it. In theory, any object will do but, like a mantra, it should be free from any psychological or emotional associations that might encourage your mind to wander.

It is traditional to use a visual tool that has some symbolic value – a picture, a geometric shape or a pattern. A selection of suitable objects is discussed opposite. You do not have to use any of these, but if you consider what makes these objects appropriate, you should apply these criteria when choosing your own.

SUITABLE VISUAL AIDS

Any object you feel drawn to will work as a visual aid, but its symbolism and associations are less important than its ability to hold your attention.

✦ A circle

This is the most simple, evocative and symbolic shape. It is a reflection of the cyclical nature of life and eternity. It expresses time, divinity, wholeness and perfection. To use this shape in meditation, draw a large black circle, about 12 inches (30 cm) in diameter, on a white background and place a white dot in the centre. Pin it to the wall at eye level. Focus on your breathing and then concentrate on the centre of the circle, while absorbing the whole image. Try to see it as a shape rather than a symbol, and experience it rather than examine it. Do not think about its symbolism or the words used to describe it: just be absorbed in looking at it. Blink when you need to and, when your attention wanders, gently return it to the circle.

✦ Other shapes

The cross and the triangle are also classic symbols used in meditation. Even before Christianity, the cross represented harmony between God and earth. The triangle symbolised perfection and the three phases of life: birth, life and death. These shapes are often combined with the circle to make more complex meditation aids known as mandalas or yantras (*see page 30*). In the early stages of your pregnancy, you might like to meditate on a cross within a circle, which signifies the process of creation.

✦ A candle

A lit candle is a traditional symbol of spiritual enlightenment. Focus on the flame and let it hold your attention. See the shape, colours, movement and brightness. If the brightness is too intense, concentrate on the tip of the flame. Close your eyes when they get tired, holding the image in your mind, and when you open them, return them to the flame.

✦ A china vase or bowl

When richly coloured and patterned, ornamental china offers plenty to look at. Also, unlike a photograph of a loved one or an image related to your pregnancy or baby, it is unlikely to have any psychological associations. Gaze at the object, take it all in, and then let your eyes explore: notice its shape, colours, lines and decoration. Allow yourself to experience it as if you were looking at it for the first time. Do not think of how it was made, or where it came from; simply gaze at the object itself.

You can use other beautiful items in a similar way. Natural objects such as a shell or starfish, flowers or a crystal are ideal because they are wonderfully captivating and complex. A tranquil picture would also work.

Traditional meditation symbols

Images are used to enhance spiritual awareness in many cultures and religions – but few are so beautiful as the mandalas and yantras of the Buddhist and Hindu traditions. These symbolise both change and permanence: they illustrate that things are now as they have always been and will always be, and affirm that everything within the universe is unified.

Mandalas, from the Sanskrit word for 'circle', are complex diagrams of the universe, based upon and within a circle. They comprise a variety of interlocking images from the natural and spiritual worlds, each detail of which has a symbolic significance that assists the meditator. Yantras are simple another form of mandala but they tend to be made of purely geometric shapes, and represent one aspect of the divine. Both have at their centre a single point, which symbolises the inner self and also God or the divine consciousness. The circles denote the cycles of life, and the whole illustrates that all life emanates from the single point at the centre.

A traditional but highly complex Tibetan mandala.

Using a traditional symbol

Mandalas and yantras are very complex so they are not always the easiest visual tool when you are learning to meditate. It may be better to start with a simple circle and move on to a mandala or yantra as you become more practised. You can also make your own mandala by filling in a circle with a selection of shapes and images of significance to you, arranged in a way that looks pleasing and balanced. Keep your eyes focused on the centre and let your mind follow the shapes, but try not to interpret it or break it down into its components, simply look at the whole image.

This geometric yantra has the universal yin-yang symbol at its centre.

Holding an image in your mind

By learning to visualise an object internally, you will find it easier to meditate anywhere and at any time: once you can hold an image in your mind, you can recall it at will from your visual memory. The following exercise is designed to improve your visualisation skills.

- *Look at an object and absorb it visually, without attempting to memorise it.*
- *Close your eyes and hold the image in your mind for as long as you can without forcing it.*
- *When it fades, open your eyes, look again at the object, and repeat the procedure. With practice you should be able to retain at least the shape of the object to use as a stimulus for future meditations.*

Visualisation

Imagining a scene can have essentially the same effect on body, mind, emotions and behaviour as perceiving that scene in reality. So picturing yourself relaxed and happy on a sun-kissed beach can actually make you feel relaxed and happy, and seeing yourself as a capable, confident mother can make you feel exactly that. Not every image has the power to do this. For greatest benefit, the image you create must be strong and you must be able to hold it for as long as you need to. You should believe in the image and be involved in it, whether it is realistic or complete fantasy. Some people find it easier to visualise than others, but you can improve your creative imagination with practice.

Using visualisation in meditation

Sit comfortably, relax and close your eyes. Conjure up an image in your mind. It could be a colour, a flower, a point of light or a beautiful scene in the country or by the sea   whatever makes you feel relaxed and happy. Use the image as your focus. Explore it, using all of your senses. If you 'see' yourself on a beach, feel the sun on your back, the sand between your toes, hear the waves lapping on the shore and smell the seaweed. Go for a swim, feel the water as it cools your skin, taste its saltiness, enjoy the weightlessness of your body floating in it. When you come out of the water, let the sun dry your skin, bask in its warmth and relax. If your mind strays from details of the scene, just bring it back and continue to explore your image for twenty minutes. At the end of your meditation, gradually allow the image to fade. Bring your attention back to the room and the present. In your own time, open your eyes, stretch gently and get up.

Visualising for health

You can overcome pain or illness by visualising the problem in any way that seems appropriate. This can be particularly useful during pregnancy. For example, if your back feels as if there is a fire at the base of your spine, use all your senses to imagine the fire scene and then visualise how you can extinguish it. Perhaps your endorphins, your body's natural painkillers, can appear as a team of tiny firemen who spray it with water. Hear the splash of the water, see the flames die down and feel the cooling sensation creep up your spine. Try to create as much detail as possible and include the body's own healing mechanisms in the image. See yourself as a healthy, active person and thank yourself for getting rid of the pain.

Visualising colour

Each colour in the spectrum has its own attributes. Focusing your mind on a particular colour can enhance your health and wellbeing. For example, visualising a wall of red can encourage fertility and energise you when you feel tired. It can ease pain or stiffness in your lower back and legs and improve circulation. It is also comforting if you feel alone or insecure. Yellow can improve digestion and concentration and foster optimism and confidence. Green is calming, reduces high blood pressure and is good for anxiety or resentment. Pale blue is relaxing, calms the nerves and soothes the emotions. It is good for insomnia, skin irritations and haemorrhoids.

Other techniques

The points of focus detailed on the previous pages work well for most people. However, there are other ways of focusing your mind during meditation. You may like to try one or more of the following techniques once you have mastered a basic skill such as breath counting or using a mantra.

Watching the body

You can use your awareness of your own body as your focus. Instead of concentrating on the movement of your breath, you zero in on sensations in the various parts of your body. Sitting in your usual position, relax completely, close your eyes and bring your awareness to your scalp. In your mind's eye focus on your scalp and notice any sensations you can feel. Do not attempt to analyse or change anything, just witness what is happening, and then move on to your face. From there, shift your attention to your neck, throat and the top of your shoulders. Then mentally focus on your arms, hands and fingers, observing even your finger nails, veins and the lines on your hands. Observe the sensations, movements and sounds of your chest and upper back, your abdomen, lower back and pelvis, then your hips, legs and finally your feet and toes. Repeat the exercise from head to toe or start at your toes and work back up the body.

Breathing in colour

This technique combines basic breathing with a visualisation of the colours of the rainbow. Start by focusing on your breathing in the normal way, counting each breath to begin with. Then visualise the colour red and breathe red into the base of your spine and out again. Make your second breath orange and breathe it in to your navel and out again. Work through the colours of the rainbow, breathing in yellow to the stomach area, green to the chest, blue to the throat, indigo to the forehead and violet to the crown of your head, and start again with red.

This makes a pleasant change from simply counting the breaths. Each colour is also believed to have a balancing effect on one of the body's seven main chakras or energy centres, which are each associated with a function of the body. Breathing each colour in to the relevant chakra may contribute to the calming restorative effect of the meditation. Throughout the meditation focus only on each colour as you see it, try not to think of its name or any other associations. You can also practise this meditation by visualising that you are breathing in sunlight, which works well outdoors on a beautiful day.

Breathe in violet if you feel confused, distraught or need to feel whole

Breathe in indigo if you have a headache, bad dreams, or insomnia

Breathe in sky blue if you are having communication problems or find it hard to care for yourself

Breathe in green if you have skin or circulation problems or little resistance to illness

Breathe in yellow if you feel fearful, stressed, have heart burn or constipation

Breathe in orange for sexual or bladder problems

Breathe in red to feel more secure, less angry, energised

Meditating with a partner

While most people meditate alone or in a class, you can also meditate with your partner or a friend. This can be particularly beneficial if you are planning or having a baby, as both of you share the same goal of enjoying a successful pregnancy and producing a happy, healthy child. Meditating together can also strengthen your relationship through having something else you can share, with the additional benefit of making both of you feel relaxed, more in harmony and bonded together in a special way.

A partner can be inspirational. He or she can lend support when your meditations seem unproductive and encourage you to practise when you may not want to. Knowing there is somebody else meditating with you can strengthen and deepen your meditation. You can also learn from shared experiences – comparing notes can reveal more about the process and help you to have realistic expectations about your achievements, although it is also important to keep something of your meditation to yourself. In some cases, focusing together on a problem can provide a solution that you may not have been able to arrive at alone.

Is it for you?

Meditating with a partner is neither better nor worse than meditating on your own. It is simply a question of what is right for you. If you are contemplating a shared meditation, here are some things to think about first:

- *Can you happily meditate alone every day or would you rarely meditate if left to your own devices?*
- *Are you easily distracted by other people; might you feel embarrassed or uncomfortable meditating in the presence of others?*
- *Is your partner genuinely willing and interested? Do not pressurise him or her into participating and do not make them feel guilty if they refuse.*

After meditating with a partner, ask yourself whether you gained something from the experience or whether you found it restricting and unproductive. And remember, shared meditation should be mutually beneficial and involve a sense of oneness with each other. You should not feel as if you are competing with your partner, so if the experience does become competitive or demanding, go back to meditating alone.

How it works

Meditating with a partner is essentially no different from meditating alone as each person's meditation is always individual. You simply share the same space and meditate at the same time. You do not need to use the same focus or aim to achieve the same goal, although this can be beneficial. For example, you could meditate together either with the view to becoming a closer family or with individual aims in mind. Even if your meditations have the same aim you might use different techniques – and if you share a technique such as visualisation, your visualisations will be different. Do not attempt to fit in with what your partner is doing, just do what is right for you at the time.

What is important is that you respect each other's needs, feelings, privacy and confidentiality. Agree on when, where and for how long you will meditate so that there are no disruptions. You should also agree on details such as incense, lighting and whether or not one of you would disturb the other by chanting aloud or breathing noisily. Working in this way with a like-minded partner once or twice a week can be beneficial, but it does not work for everyone.

Ending a meditation

Every session of meditation should end with a brief period of quiet rest. It is common to feel a little light-headed when you finish meditating, so sitting in silence will help to ground you and bring your attention back to everyday life. The purpose of meditation is not to stay in a permanently 'spaced out' state, floating above reality. In fact the reverse is true: meditation affords a short retreat from the demands of your everyday life so you can function more effectively when you return to normal consciousness. Sitting quietly and perhaps practising a simple grounding exercise helps to do this.

For basic safety reasons it is also advisable to stay seated for a minute or two at the end of your meditation. Your blood pressure will drop during a meditation so you may feel slightly dizzy if you get up too quickly or too soon. This can become more of a risk later in pregnancy when you are heavier and a fall could be dangerous, so it pays to start good habits early on.

HERE'S HOW TO FINISH SAFELY...

1 As your meditation comes to an end, stay seated with your eyes closed and gradually allow your mind to return to everyday thoughts.

2 Open your eyes and, still sitting down, just look around to familiarise yourself with the room.

3 Look at your body, move your hands, breathe deeply and stretch to get your circulation moving.

4 When you are ready, get up slowly and make sure you feel steady before getting on with your day.

5 If you still feel a little unsteady or light-headed try one of the grounding techniques described opposite.

Simple grounding techniques

Spending twenty minutes or so stilling your mind can sometimes leave you feeling 'ungrounded' or out of touch with reality. This is only a temporary feeling but there are a few easy ways to bring you back down to earth.

Sit or stand up straight and relaxed, and place your feet firmly on the ground. Breathe deeply into your abdomen and push your feet into the floor. Think of your feet sprouting roots which grow into the ground, binding you to the spot. If you are sitting in a chair, let it take your weight and get a feeling of your bottom sinking into the seat. When you stand up, stamp your feet a couple of times to get a feeling of contact with the floor.

It can also help to have a small snack or a drink when you finish meditating as this has the effect of bringing you back into reality and returning your attention to your everyday physical needs. Practical tasks have a similar ability, so you could follow your meditation by doing some cooking, shopping or gardening.

One final thought is that you may like to keep a notebook by your side to record your meditation experiences when you return to normal consciousness. In just a few lines you can note what meditation you did, what it felt like and what you got out of it. Any changes brought about by meditation are usually so gradual they are barely noticeable and a notebook is a good way of monitoring your progress.

Moving on

You are now ready to move on to the specific meditation exercises. Remember, you can adapt these exercises to suit your own needs as long as you stick to the basic meditation guidelines. Once again these are.

- *Sit comfortably.*
- *Relax completely.*
- *Focus on your chosen word / sound / breath / activity or visual image.*
- *Let everything else go.*
- *When your mind wanders, gently return it to your focus.*
- *Continue for ten to twenty minutes.*

Believe in yourself and you can do it. All it takes is commitment and practice. Good luck!

Before you conceive

*P*reparation for parenthood begins as soon as you decide that you want to become pregnant. Laying the foundations for the months ahead, both physically and emotionally, improves your chances of having a successful pregnancy and birth, a healthy baby and a happy postnatal period. This is the time to clear your body of toxic substances such as nicotine, alcohol, unnecessary drugs and poor quality foods, all of which can reduce your chances of getting pregnant and, later, could harm your baby. It is also the time to clear out emotional stresses and strains and to create within yourself a state of perfectly balanced health. When practised every day, meditation contributes to your well being at every level and forms a valuable and enjoyable part of your preconception care.

Learning how to relax

+ *Relax your mind and body*
+ *Relieve the stress that can hinder conception*
+ *Instill feelings of calm and contentment*

Deciding to have a baby, especially your first, is a major life change. Even happy events can be stressful and for some people trying to conceive can take months of anxious waiting. The thought of parenthood can be daunting as well as tremendously exciting, and it is easy for both you and your partner to feel under pressure when you want everything to go perfectly. But, often in an effort to do everything well, we forget just to relax and let nature take its course. The most basic requirement for any process of growth and healing is relaxation. As a profound state of deep relaxation, meditation returns your body to a state of balance and order and at the same time prepares it for the dynamic activity of conception and pregnancy with the minimum of stress and complications. Exercise and activity are also important in reducing stress, but thinking is the basis of all activity, so true relaxation must begin in the mind. By switching your mind off to the many thoughts that stress your body, meditation provides perfect peace, the key to good health and the ideal environment in which to conceive your child.

> *Nature knows best how to organise.*
> MAHARISHI MAHESH YOGI

How to practise this meditation

Sit comfortably in a quiet place and begin by relaxing your body. Relaxation is characterised by deep slow breaths. So, focus your attention on your abdomen and breathe in all the way down to the pit of your belly. Feel it swell as you breathe in and let it sink as you breathe out. Allow your breathing to come and go as gently as possible, and with every out-breath feel the tension drain from your muscles. Keep focusing on the rise and fall of your abdomen until your breathing establishes its own relaxed pattern.

Now close your eyes, without altering your breathing, and concentrate on the word 'Relax'. See the word written in large, chunky letters in the darkness behind your eyes, and focus only on that word. As you breathe out, say 'Relax', silently or aloud or let it escape as a whisper on your breath. As you say it, see the word spread and slump in your mind's eye as if the letters were melting; then, as you breathe in, pull it sharply back into shape. Keep focusing on the word, seeing it liquefy as you exhale and reform as you inhale. Don't impose a rhythm on your breathing: allow it to find its own pace and let all other thoughts go.

Mini meditation: an instant calmer
If you practise this meditation often your subconscious mind will quickly learn to associate the word 'Relax' with the state of relaxation so that you can relax on cue. In future times of stress, anxiety, pain or discomfort, simply taking three deep breaths and saying 'Relax' on each long, slow out-breath can bring instant comfort and relief.

> **MEDITATING FOR GOOD HEALTH**
>
> At the University of Cologne, Germany, 156 volunteers took part in a study that compared Transcendental Meditation with relaxed sitting or pretend meditation. Each participant described their moods and sensations before and after the exercise. The results showed that those who meditated were less depressed, anxious, nervous, angry, fatigued and dreamy and more relaxed, elated, active and healthy than those who pretended to meditate or simply relaxed.

Relaxation can take many forms. Losing yourself in a good book can take your mind off your worries in a way that is similar to meditation.

Boosting your fertility

Use this meditation when you want to:
◆ *Regulate your menstrual cycle and return your body to a state of natural balance*
◆ *Relieve your anxieties about getting pregnant*
◆ *Increase your chances of conception*

When trying for a baby we all hope to fall pregnant instantly. But the slightest hiccup in body functioning can make it more difficult to conceive. Doctors recommend that you increase your chances of conceiving and delivering a healthy baby by preparing for conception between three and six months in advance. You can do this by improving your physical fitness; stopping smoking, drinking alcohol and taking recreational or unnecessary prescription drugs; switching to a natural method of contraception; and reducing your exposure to environmental pollutants such as traffic fumes, aerosol sprays and paint fumes. And one of the easiest and most important ways to enhance your fertility is to improve your diet (*see opposite*).

Stress is thought to be a main cause of infertility. Your body responds to stress as it would to a threat, and in times of danger reproduction is not at the top of nature's list of priorities. Meditation can switch off that stress response, relaxing and rebalancing the body, including the hormonal and reproductive systems, so you are much more likely to become pregnant.

How to practise this meditation
This is an inspiring visualisation to perform outside if the weather is good. Sitting comfortably, relax, close your eyes and focus on your breathing.

◆ *Now imagine that you are a seed, packed with the vital energy you need to grow into a wonderful fruit-bearing tree. You are planted in the earth, feeling safe, peaceful and nurtured. You are tranquil, yet*

EATING FOR FERTILITY

You and your partner should try to make the following improvements to your diet six months before you plan to conceive.

- Filter all water and aim to drink two litres a day. Avoid coffee.
- Eat fresh wholefoods with at least five portions of fruit and vegetables a day; choose organic produce where possible.

- Have your vitamin and mineral levels checked. Take a high quality multivitamin and mineral supplement, which contains iron, zinc, magnesium and vitamins C, E and B complex to enhance your fertility.
- Take 400 mcg of folic acid a day to reduce the risk of your baby developing neural tube defects.

The fertility boosting diet must include a wide variety of fresh foods. Fruit and vegetables provide antioxidant vitamins essential for reproductive function in men and women. Milk, seafood and nuts provide zinc, needed for sperm production and healthy foetal development.

eager to grow. Above you is a glimmer of sunlight and you feel an urge to grow towards it. As you start to stretch upwards you feel your energy begin to move and you push out roots to give you a firm foundation. Slowly you grow towards the sun, feeling it warming and welcoming you. Gentle raindrops refresh and nourish as you start to grow tall and strong. First leaves, then blossom appear on your branches, making you look and feel healthy and radiant. As a soft breeze causes the flower petals to fall to the ground, all your cares float off with them and you feel peaceful and happy. In place of the blossom, fruit begins to grow. It looks healthy, delicious and is growing bigger all the time. Enjoy the pleasantly heavy sensation of this natural burden, congratulate yourself for having produced it and delight in the knowledge that you have achieved your purpose.

Positive images for moments of doubt

If you are worrying about whether you will be able to get pregnant, try creating such a strong, positive image in your mind's eye that it pushes out any doubts or anxieties. Picture yourself, your partner and your beautiful baby together and happy in a special safe place. See the image so clearly that your brain accepts it as fact and tells your body to make it a reality.

Making the most of fertility treatments

Use this meditation when you want to:
- ◆ Trust in your ability to conceive
- ◆ Make a decision about whether or not to embark on fertility treatment
- ◆ Take more pleasure in the present
- ◆ Find the resources to cope with stressful procedures

The main meditation in this section is a mindfulness meditation. Mindfulness, which is based on Buddhist principles, means being in the moment and its purpose is to increase your appreciation of everything life has to offer. Trying unsuccessfully to get pregnant can mean you spend too much time regretting decisions you made in the past, worrying and dreaming about the future, and never really taking pleasure in the present.

> *No matter how stressed you are by ongoing events, you will still appreciate small moments if you remain mindful.*
> DR ALICE DOMAR, DIRECTOR OF THE WOMEN'S HEALTH PROGRAMME, HARVARD MEDICAL SCHOOL

Having fertility treatment can leave you anticipating every treatment and awaiting test results in a state of almost permanent anxiety. It can also make you feel stressed and unhappy in your relationship or as if your life is 'on hold'. Often the best way to deal with fertility problems and increase your chances of conception is to take your mind off it completely. Rather than long for happiness in the future, just focus on how wonderful and blessed you can feel right at this moment. Try to do activities as a couple, spend time with friends and allow yourself treats. Romantic weekends away or quiet time on your own will not be easy to arrange when you have a baby to look after, so enjoy them now. Becoming mindful of everyday events such as baking a cake or going for a swim can also be incredibly therapeutic. Being engrossed in a task anchors you in the present, blots out anxieties and enables you to take pleasure in your life right now.

How to practise this meditation

Begin by sitting comfortably and focus on your breathing. Just be aware of the movement of your breath and the way it enters and leaves your body. Worries, anxieties, hopes and dreams will continue to flood your mind so just sit quietly and watch each thought come and go. Be aware of how your thought process works, how different ideas keep appearing and disappearing and vying for attention. Observe the process but try not to get carried along with the thoughts; if you do, just return to observing your breath and how it is moving at this moment in your body. Do not be too hard on yourself if you do lose concentration, however, just accept that it happens, let your thoughts go, and return to your breath and the present. As you end your meditation know that at any time you can let go of your worries about the future and just be relaxed in the present.

Mini meditation: during treatment

At times of particular stress, anxiety, fear or pain, you can remain calm by practising a mini mindfulness meditation. Just find an object of interest in the car, waiting room or in the clinic where you are being treated and focus on it to the exclusion of all else. It could be a plant, a picture or the view through a window. Don't stare at it, just relax, half close your eyes, let your breathing find a slow, natural rhythm and explore the object in such detail that there is no room for anxieties to nudge their way in.

What worked for me

When I discovered I was infertile I felt angry, sorry for myself and worthless. I've never really agreed with fertility treatment, but I was so desperate I was prepared to reject my own principles. In quiet moments I would sit down, empty my mind and ask for guidance. Gradually, I thought less about babies and more about how blessed I was in other areas of my life, how happy I felt and how much I was loved. I'd still like to have a child, but I no longer feel bereft.

Focusing on your partnership

Use this meditation when you want to:
◆ *Strengthen your bond with your partner*
◆ *Increase your enjoyment of the present*
◆ *Improve your capacity to love and be loved*

Most people want to have children together because they love each other. It is all too easy, however, to get overly focused on conceiving. Baby-centred lovemaking can become more of a chore than a spontaneous act of pleasure and passion, so be sure to keep a loving physical relationship alive *throughout* your reproductive cycle.

If you've been trying to have a baby for some time, try not to become too fraught. Remember that while each menstrual period may seem like your body is betraying *you*, it is also disappointing for your partner. He may feel that his virility is being questioned, or that he is being treated like a baby-making machine rather than the man that you love. It's important not to lose sight of the closeness between you. Focus on the fact that you are together because you love each other, and not because you would make perfect parents. Encourage that love to grow by making time for each other, appreciating each other's qualities, continuing to enjoy each other's company, and meditating to retain a sense of calm and generosity.

> *Love is not looking into each other's eyes; it is looking together in the same direction.*
>
> ANTOINE DE SAINT-EXUPÉRY

Couples who meditate together claim to enjoy greater harmony and intimacy. But even meditating alone may strengthen your relationship by focusing your attention on improving yourself, rather than trying to find fault with your partner. Meditation also encourages the growth of happiness within yourself. People who are happy, tolerant and loving find it difficult to be thoughtless or quarrelsome.

Mindful loving

Mindfulness is about being completely absorbed in any activity you do. Being mindful of your love-making lets you savour each moment of togetherness with your partner and takes your mind off baby worries. Use all your senses, emotions and thoughts to experience each moment of your love-making. It will increase your enjoyment of all that life has to offer, strengthen your attachment to your partner and relieve anxieties about the future.

How to practise this meditation

This meditation fosters the growth of unconditional love by focusing on the heart. Place a rose bud or any other flower bud front of you. Sit down, relax as normal and look at the flower with half-closed eyes. Focus on it in a relaxed way and let all other thoughts float out of your mind.

◆ *Study the flower and as you become more aware of its shape, colour and beauty imagine it growing in your heart. Close your eyes and visualise it inside you, waiting to be coaxed into bloom by the power of love. When it does flower, it will radiate love all around you. Keep focusing on the bud and see it gradually unfold its petals and spread out, little by little, to take up the whole space of your heart. Eventually, you can see nothing else because your heart has become the flower. Its fragrance is like the scent of love. It permeates all the cells and tissues of your body and wafts out through your pores. The perfume envelops you and radiates from you. Your heart is full of love, you feel loved and loving, complete and serene. Continue to sit for a few minutes, focusing on your heart flower, enjoying its fragrance and radiance before opening your eyes.*

Mini visualisation: in times of crisis

When you feel angry with or hurt by your partner, try the following Buddhist technique to instill love in place of bitterness. Visualise an image of yourself being superimposed on your partner and hold the image for as long as you can. You should find it difficult to stay upset when you see parts of yourself in him.

Establishing healthy habits

Use this meditation when you want to:
+ *Replace bad habits with better ones*
+ *Reduce the stress and symptoms of withdrawal*
+ *Purify your body*

We all know that it is unwise to smoke, drink alcohol or use drugs during pregnancy, but these bad habits can adversely affect your fertility too. Tobacco, for example, contains many toxins which, among many other harmful effects, lower levels of the reproductive hormone oestrogen in women and reduce sperm quality in men. Alcohol can depress a man's ability to perform sexually and damage sperm production; it can also increase the risks of miscarriage.

Quitting cigarettes, alcohol and drugs will not only enhance your fertility, it will also leave you in better health for pregnancy and parenthood. But giving up is rarely easy, even when you have a good reason. Habits are comforting, not necessarily because you Like doing them but because the very act of doing something repeatedly makes you feel secure. Kicking one habit can leave a huge gap in your life that you feel desperate to fill with another. Yet meditation, which you practise twice a day, can also be thought of as a habit, and many meditators naturally tend to give up bad habits. Researchers at the University of Michigan medical school found that 71–100 per cent of people who meditated for more than two years smoked significantly fewer cigarettes than they had done before, and 57 per cent stopped completely. They also found that 40 per cent of one group of meditators gave up alcohol within six months of taking up the practice, and 60 per cent had given up within two years. So it helps to think that you are replacing your bad habits with a much better one that will enhance your fertility and improve the health of you and your baby.

How to practise this meditation

Sit or lie down comfortably in a quiet space. Relax and start to breathe in through your nose, deep into your lungs and abdomen, and out through your mouth. Spend some time finding a level of deep breathing that feels comfortable. Close your eyes and be aware only of the movement and rhythm of your breath.

After a few minutes, visualise the air you are breathing in as the cleanest, most healing white light you have ever seen. As you inhale this purifying light, see it fill up your lungs and imagine it spreading out all around your body, cleansing and healing every cell with which it comes into contact. See it purify and protect your uterus in particular. Continue to focus on this image, while also imagining your out-breath moving up from the base of your belly. As it moves up, see it sweeping all the toxins out of your abdomen and lungs. See the old stained breath leaving your body to be replaced by the clean white light. Gradually see the air you exhale become cleaner, until it is as white as the air you are breathing in. Your body is now filled with pure, healing air. Breathe this white light in and out for several minutes. When you are ready, open your eyes and get up slowly.

Mini meditation: in moments of temptation

If you feel like you want a cigarette or a drink, stop, relax your shoulders, and take a deep breath into your belly. As you breathe out, slowly let your shoulders drop further and say the words, 'I am clean and pure'. Repeat the exercise any time the desire creeps back to the front of your mind.

FIVE GOOD REASONS TO QUIT BAD HABITS NOW

✦ Pregnant women who smoke are more likely to miscarry, bleed during pregnancy and give birth to premature or small babies.

✦ Babies born to smokers have reduced immunity to infections in the first year and are at greater risk of cot death (sudden infant death syndrome).

✦ Children of smokers have been shown to have reduced intellectual capacity and may suffer malformations such as a cleft palate.

✦ Drinking heavily during pregnancy can restrict your baby's growth, cause mental retardation, physical deformities, problems of the heart and nervous system and possibly still birth.

✦ Stop using recreational drugs and consult your doctor if you take prescribed medication. Certain drugs can reduce your fertility and later, during pregnancy, cause foetal abnormalities or affect your health.

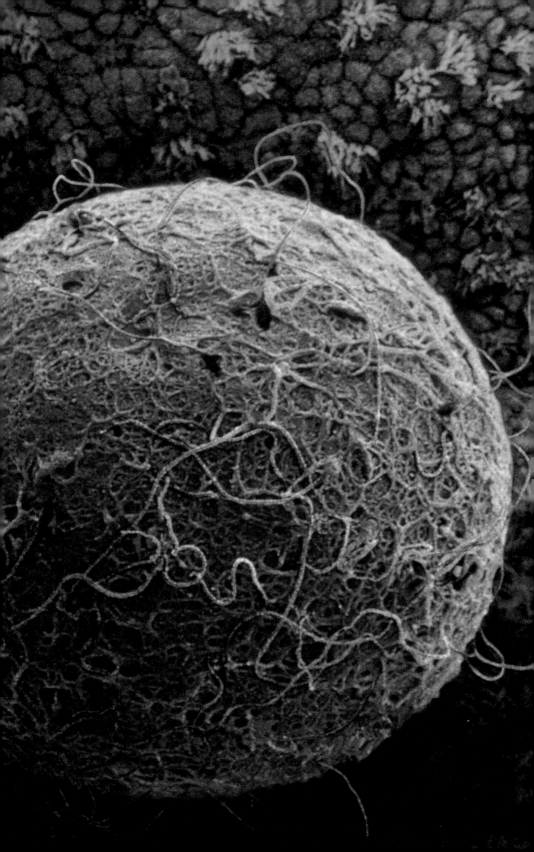

The first trimester

The first twelve weeks of your pregnancy, known as the first trimester, can be among the most thrilling in your life. Although your body may not look different, you are almost certain to feel different — both physically and emotionally — thanks to the enormous changes taking place inside you. The first three months are the most significant in terms of foetal development, so it is particularly important to nurture yourself and your baby during these crucial early weeks. The meditations in this section are designed to help you make the most of this amazing time and give your baby the best start in life!

Welcoming the new life inside you

Use this meditation when you want to:

+ *Celebrate the creation of a new life*
+ *Start bonding with your child*
+ *Accept you're pregnant even if there are no visible signs*

Congratulations – you're pregnant! Whether this is your first child or your third, the excitement of discovering that you have created and are nurturing a new life is a truly wonderful experience. Some women sail through pregnancy without giving much thought to what is happening inside them. And yet there is more than just a tiny embryo developing, day-by-day, inside the uterus: pregnancy represents the beginning of the growth of a unique individual. It also signifies the start of a whole new phase in the lives of you and your partner.

Celebrate this new person and the fact that you are pregnant. Treat yourself and your baby as a very special team. Although, at this early stage of pregnancy, you probably won't yet be fully aware of your baby, many changes are taking place within you. Affirming your baby's presence and welcoming this new member of the family will help you to focus on these changes and make parenthood more real to you. This pre-birth bonding is the first step to forming a lifelong attachment with your child.

The object of the following body scan meditation is to raise your awareness of and emotional attachment to the child growing within you, and to welcome and embrace his or her presence with both your body and mind.

How to practise this meditation

Find a place that is quiet and comfortable – you may want to choose a spot that becomes your 'sanctuary' during pregnancy, where you can spend time on your own without fear of interruption. Make sure you are in a comfortable position that you can hold without difficulty for the duration of the meditation.

Start by gently shaking out the tensions in your muscles and then ease yourself into a lying position. Once you feel settled, concentrate on your breathing until it is slow and calm. Now divide your body into seven distinct sections: scalp and forehead; face and neck; shoulders, arms and hands; chest and back; diaphragm and solar plexus; the belly; hips, legs and feet. This will allow you to focus intimately on each one in turn.

Beginning at the top of your head and working slowly down to the tips of your toes, concentrate all your attention on each section for the duration of a few breaths, clenching the muscles in each part of your body on the inhalation and releasing the tension as you breathe out. Focus on the flow of your breathing, especially in and out of your abdomen, and be aware of the sensations in your breasts and belly. This will make you more aware of the subtle changes that are taking place in your body.

To give yourself a more concrete focus, you could use a visual aid. Before you start your meditation, draw a circle with a dot in the middle to represent life and its eternity (*see page 29*). Now, without analysing the circle or its meaning, let your eyes move over the image, and familiarise yourself with it. Try shutting your eyes and keeping the image of the circle in your mind. Continue to be aware of your breathing but don't count your breaths as this shifts your focus of attention. Accept any thoughts that arise, but just let them float away, concentrating only on the circle. Remain aware of the physical sensations of the meditation as you focus on the circle, so that your baby's presence becomes linked with the way you feel in your body. The meditation should last approximately fifteen minutes. The first few times you try this you could set a kitchen timer or alarm clock to let you know when it is time gently to open your eyes and come out of the meditation.

What worked for me

I was amazed by the intense emotions, insights, vivid dreams, fears, and aspirations of pregnancy. Keeping a journal was a great way to explore these feelings, and is a wonderful chronicle for the future. At times when I felt troubled by unresolved issues from the past, I used it to vent my emotions without worrying about how other people might react. I wrote what and when I liked, without trying to write something every day

Encouraging the healthy development of your baby

Use this meditation when you want to:

◆ Find the strength to give up things that are not good for your baby

◆ Banish worries about a particular aspect of your pregnancy

◆ Relax your mind and body, which will benefit your baby

Every parent dreams of a healthy baby – it is the most natural wish in the world to want all to be right with your child. Well, the first twelve weeks are the most important in your baby's development, so you will want to ensure that you are doing all that you can for your unborn child.

From the moment of conception, each of your baby's tiny body parts starts working to its own timetable of evolution: the heart forms between the third and sixth weeks in utero, the buds that will develop into the limbs begin forming between the fourth and seventh weeks, and by the end of the first trimester, your child's basic brain structure and a rudimentary nervous system will also be in place.

In order to thrive during this crucial time, your baby needs to grow in its own small sanctuary. And in many ways the preservation of that sanctuary is in your hands. It is important to avoid stressful situations, to abstain from harmful substances such as alcohol and nicotine, and to nurture your child by eating a balanced diet. However, during the emotional upheavals of these early weeks, you may be particularly tempted by the props you used to rely on in times of stress. Meditation can help you resist these cravings, and provide an alternative way to relax.

Meditating each day ensures that you have the time alone that you need to relax. It also helps you focus positively on the healthy development of your baby. Rest assured that time spent on yourself is well spent – by looking after yourself and your own needs you will be protecting your baby and doing everything you can to encourage a successful pregnancy for both of you. This meditation shows you how to direct your attention – through sight, sound and smell – to the garden growing within you, allowing the power of the positive to guide your baby through this very important time.

How to practise this meditation

Choose some place, perhaps in the garden if you have one or a quiet spot in the park, where you can see or hear signs of nature to give you a sense of the life growing within you. If you are a novice meditator, you may find being outside too distracting when you are trying to focus. If this is the case, try sitting instead in the room that that you have chosen as your sanctuary; this will have a calming influence that helps you focus. You may like to have a vase of fragrant flowers with you as you meditate.

> *There is no need to go to the garden of flowers. Within your body is a garden.*
> VERSES OF KABIR

Once you are comfortable, close your eyes and focus on the rhythm of your breathing by counting each in-breath. Concentrate on the changes in your body as you inhale and exhale. Think of your breaths as the unseen but very real presence of your baby – you cannot see it, but you know it is there every minute of the day. When your breathing has become balanced and regular, start using it to complement an affirmation. Choose one of the affirmations below, or alternatively use one of your own. Let the knowledge that each breath is carrying oxygen to your baby support the positive message of the affirmation. Practise repeating the phrase until it's instantly soothing; you can also use it as a mini meditation when you're out and about, to calm any nagging fears as they arise.

* *I am the carrier of a healthy growing baby*
* *My body is a safe haven for my baby*
* *My baby is safe and well within me*
* *My baby is a unique human being*

Using an affirmation creates a mental and physical state that not only encourages your child's healthy development but also calms you down and counteracts any negative thoughts that cross your mind. It's a way of confirming that you want the best for your baby and of blocking any distracting thoughts. It should pervade your mind until it's no longer just a collection of words but a part of you.

Coping with the fear of miscarriage

Use this meditation when you want to:
◆ *Calm any worries about losing your baby*
◆ *Acknowledge and express your feelings about a previous miscarriage*
◆ *Learn to look to the future rather than the past*

The pleasure of pregnancy can sometimes be marred by fears such as that of losing your child. This is a worry common to many mothers-to-be and is connected with anxiety about having a healthy baby. These fears may be especially acute if you have experienced a miscarriage in the past; in this case it is even more important to relax and stay calm during the early months of pregnancy if you are to enjoy it fully.

Miscarriage occurs when the foetus spontaneously aborts before the twenty-eighth week. Usually due to an abnormality of the foetus, it is most common in the first few weeks of pregnancy, and frequently happens before the pregnancy has been confirmed or even suspected. It may help to think of miscarriage as nature's way of ending a pregnancy that, for whatever reason, cannot go full term. It is important, therefore, not to blame yourself – doctors say that if a miscarriage is going to happen there is almost nothing you can do about it.

The power of positive thinking

A confident attitude can help you tackle your fears and remain relaxed during the first three months of pregnancy when you are at the highest risk of miscarriage. If you have lost a previous pregnancy, it may be difficult to keep calm, but remember that the majority of women who have had a miscarriage go on to have normal, healthy pregnancies. Meditate on the loss of your child and try not to shut out your grief. Accepting your feelings will help you look forward to the new life growing within you.

Sitting quietly and concentrating on your breathing is an excellent way of calming down both mind and body. The way in which you breathe reflects your emotional state. When you are feeling over-emotional, your stress levels rise and your breathing becomes shallow and hurried, which in turn increases your sense of strain. Conversely, as your breathing slows and becomes more relaxed, your mind will become calm and the tension will ease out of your body.

How to practise this meditation

Choose a place you find reassuring, where you feel tranquil and secure, and find a comfortable position that allows you to breathe freely and easily. Spend a few moments thinking about your body and consciously make tiny adjustments to your posture to ease any areas of tension.

Allow the muscles in your chest and abdomen to loosen to give your breath room to move around your body. Let your breathing be spontaneous – think about it without trying to breathe 'correctly'. Keep focused by counting each inhalation. If your concentration wanders and you lose count, gently bring your attention back to your breathing without getting annoyed. If you feel sleepy, concentrate more intently on the sensations in your body – how has your breathing changed? What emotions are you experiencing?

As you relax the physical and mental defences of everyday life, your fears and grief may surface. Acknowledge painful or fearful emotions but let them leave your body with each exhalation. Use this time of quietness to say goodbye if you have experienced a previous loss. Now focus on the future and concentrate your thoughts on the new baby within. Put your hands on your belly and visualise the comforting protective environment of your uterus. Imagine all the nutrients your growing foetus needs travelling across the placenta and down the umbilical cord from you to your baby. Feel how attached the two of you are, and reassure yourself that everything will be fine.

DANGER SIGNS

If you experience vaginal bleeding at any stage during your pregnancy, especially if it is accompanied by pain, you should seek prompt medical attention.

- Go to bed or lie down somewhere comfortable and wait for the doctor.
- Prop your feet up on some pillows to keep your legs and hips raised.
- Don't take any alcohol, painkillers or any other medication until you have consulted a doctor.
- Use a cold compress or fan to keep cool. Above all, remember that although vaginal bleeding occurs in a quarter of all pregnancies, most proceed healthily to full term.

Conserving your energy

Use this meditation when you want to:
- ✦ Overcome *feelings of tiredness*
- ✦ *Concentrate your energies, particularly if you notice you are easily distracted*
- ✦ *Relax and take it easy without feeling guilty*

In the first three months of pregnancy, your body has a hard time keeping up physically with the mental excitement you're experiencing. Once the first flush of elation is over, you may feel totally exhausted and just want to curl up and sleep for hours. This is to be expected: your body is having to cope with enormous changes, even if you are not yet aware of them, which means it's working a lot harder than usual.

Don't feel you have failed because you're not able to do as much as you could before you were pregnant. Prioritise your tasks, doing only what is essential. Let some of your commitments drop – time to yourself is important for the welfare of you and your unborn child. Plan your routine around moments of stillness: this slows your metabolism, relaxes your mind and recoups lost energy.

How to practise this meditation

A body scan is a good way of becoming sensitised to what your body is telling you it needs. Find a comfortable sitting posture that keeps your back straight: in a chair, on the floor or a cushion, maybe with your back against the wall. Rest your hands in your lap, close your eyes, and take a few moments to relax your breathing.

Beginning at the top of your head and working down, note the tension in each area before consciously clenching and relaxing it. Ask yourself questions such as, 'What is causing my shoulders to feel tired and how can I try to change this?' As you complete the scan, consider your priorities and ask yourself what you need to achieve today and what you need to concentrate your energies on. Although this may take practice, trust your judgement, let your mind ask the questions and the answers will come naturally to you.

To improve your energy levels, create a picture of yourself doing the things you want to do and having the energy to do them in a positive, relaxed way. Be flexible and realistic – one day you may just want to survive eight hours at work, while another you may have specific tasks you'd like to fulfil. You can either devise a visualisation of your own, or try one of the following:

- *Imagine energy coursing through your body like a waterfall, from the top of your head, down to your toes. You feel the energy within motivating you to do everything you want, to overcome every obstacle and feel satisfied with each job done.*
- *See yourself in your work environment. You are busy, but can work out what needs to be addressed first and what can wait till later. You are confident and feel happy and rewarded by your work.*

Mini meditation: slowing down

Constantly rushing and trying to fit too many things into one day is the quickest way to exhaustion. Frenetic action not only increases your metabolic rate and stress levels, it also wastes precious energy. This exercise will help you take things easy.

Choose an everyday chore like getting dressed, and perform every activity consciously slower, leaving yourself extra time so you don't feel hurried. Focus closely on every movement you make. Notice the pace at which you open the ward-robe and pull out a hanger – is the way you move jerky and awkward or smooth and relaxed? What is your breathing like? Enjoy the passing sensations – the feel of the fabric, the sound of a zipper being fastened, the smell of a freshly laundered blouse. Keep your mind concentrated on experiencing the present and don't allow yourself to worry about all the things you think you 'should' be doing. Do this for a few days running and notice the difference.

Overcoming early physical complaints

Use this meditation when you want to:

◆ *Dispel fears that you'll never stop feeling sick*

◆ *Remain relaxed, in spite of physical discomfort*

◆ *Accept your complaints, not fight them*

◆ *Free your mind to focus on more positive aspects of your pregnancy*

Many women suffer from morning sickness, heartburn or tender breasts during the first trimester, but it is important not to let these physical discomforts dominate the early months of your pregnancy. Try to think positively: these ailments are your body's natural response to the changes happening within it and a good sign that your pregnancy is progressing well. You can also think of them as proof that there is a new life growing within you. You may find this difficult, especially if you have very much wanted to be pregnant and now find you feel sick all the time, but be reassured that these complaints won't last forever: by the second trimester you will be glowing with health and energy.

A strong belief that you will be well can have an enormous effect on how you feel; it can help you remain relaxed during discomfort, and foster a positive attitude toward your symptoms. What's more, meditating can physically relieve many complaints by regulating your breathing and other body functions.

How to practise this meditation

Choose a comfortable place with plenty of cushions. If you are feeling sick, uncomfortable or your breasts are very tender, wear loose clothing and lie down to do this exercise.

Focusing on your breathing can be particularly useful in overcoming nausea. Begin by breathing normally and count each out-breath until you reach ten. Then repeat the process, counting the in-breaths. This will help

UNDERSTANDING MORNING SICKNESS

About half of all pregnant women experience morning sickness to some degree. Most sufferers find their symptoms are worst during the first trimester and improve considerably, if not completely, thereafter.

The exact cause of morning sickness still remains something of a mystery, but experts believe it is linked to the high levels of hormones travelling through the maternal bloodstream, and particularly of progesterone, which is produced within the ovaries during the first 12–14 weeks of pregnancy. Blood sugar levels are also affected during pregnancy and if they fall, for instance after a long evening without food or if you're not eating enough, this may cause nausea.

Although it often occurs in the morning, the nausea can last all day. In the most severe (but rare) cases, severe vomiting can lead to hospitalisation due to loss of fluids. To diminish the effects of morning sickness:

✦ Eat little and often.

✦ Avoid spicy, strong-smelling foods.

✦ Eat high-carbohydrate foods such as potatoes and cereals.

✦ Avoid cigarette smoke and rich perfumes.

you concentrate your mind on your breathing and away from your symptoms. As you focus on each breath, think of a time when you felt wonderful and energetic. Concentrate on feeling good and let the feeling wash over you, dispersing any discomfort.

Use a visualisation to turn your discomfort into a positive experience or to rid yourself of it completely. When you are in doubt or pain, it may help to recall the story about Buddha who, while sitting in meditation during an attack from an enemy army, turned the missiles falling all around him into harmless, sweet-scented flowers. Personalise one of the following to suit your needs:

◆ *If you're suffering from tender breasts, imagine that your baby is born. You are holding your baby to your breast and the tenderness you are feeling is because your baby is feeding and you are the sole provider of his or her daily needs. Your baby only has eyes for you and is warm and secure in your arms.*

◆ *If you're suffering from morning sickness, visualise a television screen showing your body. Notice that the pain-free areas are shining with a white light. Then concentrate on those aching parts you want to heal. Imagine the light slowly expanding so that gradually your whole body is bathed in it and you can rejoice in your healthy, glowing body.*

Finding peace of mind

Use this meditation when you want to:
◆ *Feel in control of your emotions*
◆ *Accept changes that will inevitably happen*
◆ *Cope with sudden tearful outbursts*
◆ *Deal with feelings of uncertainty about your relationships*
◆ *Acknowledge your need to be mothered*

Pregnancy is a very challenging time emotionally and it isn't always easy to deal with the tremendous emotional highs and lows you will be experiencing. One minute you may feel elated about the future, the next depressed about how your life is going to change and whether you will be able to cope with a young baby. Genuine fears and worries can be exacerbated by your fluctuating hormones, which can have a depressive effect similar to that occurring before a period.

> *Silence the chaos within.*
> DR HERBERT BENSON

Furthermore, feelings that would usually be suppressed surface far more easily when you are pregnant, so use this time as a good opportunity to deal with any unresolved issues in your life, for instance with your partner. Resolving old conflicts will help you embrace the new life within you and the changes it will bring to your life. Accepting that your life will be different and that it's alright to have conflicting feelings is the first step to achieving peace of mind.

Meditation can help you calm your inner turmoil, acknowledge your negative emotions and, by thinking positively about them, ultimately learn to let them go. Contemplating your past and future life will help you be more accepting of yourself and your ability to be a parent. If you are finding it difficult to put your finger on exactly what you are upset about, focus your mind and use music and mantras to help you deal effectively with each change in your mood.

How to practise this meditation

Music is wonderful for calming turbulent emotions and soothing fears. Meditation heightens all your senses so an aural focus is a particularly good way to still confused or conflicting thoughts, and help you put things into perspective.

What worked for me

If I was feeling over-emotional and finding it difficult to concentrate, aromatherapy candles helped me achieve calm.

If you feel yourself mentally chasing your own tail, take time out and find a place where you can be alone and listen to a favourite piece of music. This way you can create an oasis of tranquillity anywhere – even if this just means sitting in the car with your eyes shut, the doors closed, and the music playing. You can use any type of non-vocal music: choose something that is meaningful to you – uplifting, inspirational or calming, depending on your mood.

A few of my favourites were lavender, which is calming and therapeutic; neroli, to relax and reassure myself; and sandalwood, to build confidence. Always be sure to check that a particular fragrance is suitable for a pregnant woman to use.

As you listen, focus on how the music resonates in your body and what effect it has on your physical state. Concentrate on the fact that being calm is doing your body good too. If the music arouses mental associations and images, accept them and use them to extend your meditation. However, don't allow yourself to be distracted: ask yourself every so often if you are still following the music and gently bring yourself back if your mind wanders. You may also wish to use an affirmation to support the positive feelings that the music arouses. Try one of the following affirmations, or adapt one to suit your mood:

* *I accept myself as I am*
* *I am aware of what comes into my mind
and keeps me from feeling peaceful*
* *My family will be happy and healthy*

If you find that you are distracted by negative thoughts, try thinking of them as 'roadblocks' to peace of mind. Use the affirmation to acknowledge these mental obstacles and think positively about yourself to move beyond them. Spend a few quiet moments at the end of the meditation to appreciate how your anxiety has been quieted.

The prospect of single motherhood

Use this meditation when you want to:

◆ *Quell feelings of loneliness*
◆ *Find courage to feel positive about the future*
◆ *Boost your self-confidence and believe in the strength of your convictions*
◆ *Find inner peace and contentment*

For many women, the early signs of pregnancy are a very exciting time – but this period can also be scary and isolating. As a single mother-to-be, you may be worried about your ability to cope. You will really be looking within yourself during the first trimester, pulling on resources and emotions that you may not have known you had, and learning to be strong for the sake of your child and whatever the future brings. Remember, being a single mother does not mean you are alone. Lean on your family and friends for the support you need. You may also like to think about choosing a particular person who can accompany you on your antenatal check-ups and later act as your birth partner.

> *Nothing in the world is single;*
> *All things, by a law divine,*
> *in one spirit meet and mingle.*
> PERCY SHELLEY, LOVE'S PHILOSOPHY

It is important that you use your energy positively, concentrate on the happy aspects of life, and allow yourself to let go of the things that are really not important. This meditation will strengthen your belief in yourself and help quell your doubts. Bringing a child into the world on your own is something very special; it takes great courage and strength. Celebrate this courage and think positively about your pregnancy. You will have a very intimate relationship with your child, who will be dependent on you for love, guidance and protection throughout his or her life.

How to practise this meditation

Choose a place where you feel secure and comfortable and that inspires you with feelings of capability and courage. Take a few moments to become calm, using a technique that works for you – such as counting your breaths – before focusing on a visualisation. Close your eyes and concentrate on all the things you can do as a mother, now and in the years to come. If you are experiencing hurt, resentment or anger, let these feelings enter your mind but then let them pass.

Visualisations can help you to love yourself and accept the situation you are in now. If you are wondering whether you have done the right thing, use a visualisation to accept that this is the road you are on and that it is the route to a positive life ahead.

◆ *Imagine yourself walking along a beautiful, tree-lined road. You are walking slowly but assuredly. Occasionally there is a pothole or a rock to climb over or around, but you see these obstacles coming and easily deal with them. You are not tired walking, but full of energy, with a spring in your step, because you know you are walking towards something beautiful and eternally fulfilling.*

Mini meditation: in moments of self-doubt

Mantras are particularly useful when you are struck by fears. Choose a phrase that is easy to remember so you can bring it to mind whenever you feel the need to reassure yourself. A mantra could be a short, meaningful phrase that has affirmative associations for you; if you are religious, why not try a phrase with spiritual significance; or you may prefer a simple monosyllable such as 'Om', that is valuable for the soothing quality of the sound itself. Invent one that works for you or try one of the following:

* *Healthy am I; Happy am I; Holy am I*
* *Om mani padme hum (the great Tibetan Buddhist mantra, meaning 'Hail to the jewel in the lotus')*
* *We two are special*

Use them to help you at any time: chanting under your breath when you are alone, or silently if you're in company.

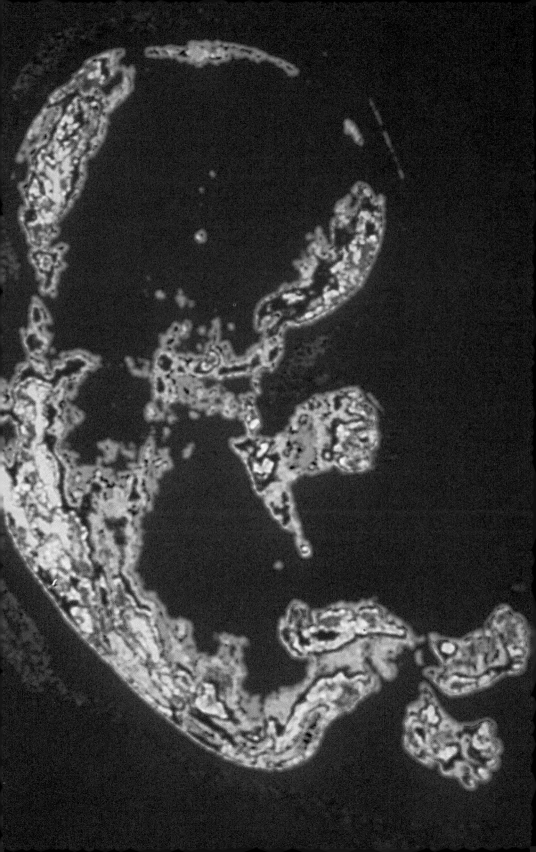

The second trimester

This trimester represents the next sixteen weeks of your pregnancy. It is often the easiest and most enjoyable of the three trimesters. You'll find you're less tired and have more energy to deal with all the changes taking place — so make the most of this wonderful time! At the beginning you will notice that your abdomen is becoming more rounded and your waistline is starting to disappear. But by week twenty-eight, your waistline will have completely gone, you'll have probably gained around 6 kg and have a beautiful big bump in front of you. Nurture your baby and yourself by eating well, getting plenty of rest and looking after your body to prevent problems such as backache and swollen ankles.

Partners preparing for parenthood

Use this meditation when you want to:

✦ *Subdue concerns about how a baby will affect you as individuals and as a partnership*

✦ *Work together as a team*

✦ *Reassure one another of your love*

✦ *Banish fears about your partner's involvement*

Now that you are in your second trimester and, at last, the visible bump of your baby is beginning to show, you and your partner may start to think more about the reality of how parenthood is going to affect you. The

Having a child together is a natural progression of your relationship, so be sure to share your baby's first kicks.

excitement you both feel at becoming parents is bound to be accompanied by some worries. You may fear your loss of independence or experience sudden panics that your partner may not want to be as involved as you would like, while he may be concerned about being left out after the new arrival or how he will manage financially while you are not working.

Focusing on your togetherness as a couple and being open about your feelings will stand you in good stead during the upheaval – as well as joy – of having a newborn in the home. Involve your partner as much as you can: together read about what is happening in the week-by-week development of your baby and when you feel its first movements at around twenty weeks, let him experience this too by holding your belly. See yourselves as a team, building a secure environment for your unborn child. And, particularly importantly, accept now that there will be new priorities in your lives and that your relationship is bound to change, mostly for the better. Learning now how to resolve conflicts as they arise will undoubtedly help you cope later once your little one has arrived.

How to practise this meditation

Meditating together is a wonderful experience, as it is a special time when you are sitting quietly and focusing on the future with your child. Don't expect to experience the same effects as each other every time, but the longer you practise, the more synchronised you may become. The following meditation can be used by both you and your partner. Unless you are practised meditators, you may find it difficult to concentrate if one or both of you are chanting aloud, as it is easy to be distracted. So meditating silently may work best.

Find a place where you both feel comfortable – you may need a chair for support while your partner is happier on the floor. Start by concentrating on your breathing, letting it become slow and regular and feel the tension ease out of your body. Be aware of your partner's presence, but don't let it interfere with what you want to focus on. Use a favourite piece of music – non-vocal is the least distracting – to create a calm ambience and help fill the room with sound other than your partner's breathing.

Now, create your own images of how you would like life to be once the baby is born. You, for instance, may want to focus on being an active mother but still a competent individual. Imagine yourself lovingly looking after your child, but also seeing friends, reading a good book, commenting on the day's international news. Your partner may wish to concentrate more on seeing you all together as family, with himself taking an active role in helping with the baby and taking control when necessary, for instance, to give you a rest. You should both visualise time together when it is just the two of you – all new parents need to maintain their own unique relationship as well as being together as a family.

Do this for 15 minutes and then talk about what you have visualised, any blockages you came up against when creating your picture and how you might overcome these next time you meditate together.

Beating backache and other ailments

Use this meditation when you want to:

◆ *Think positively about your body's reaction to pregnancy*

◆ *Try to prevent problems from occurring*

◆ *Deal calmly with physical complaints if they do arise*

Now that the fatigue and sickness of the early weeks have worn off, you will probably find that you are feeling a lot better and have more energy to cope with everyday tasks. Nevertheless, you may still experience a few minor problems.

One of the most common ailments of the second trimester is backache, caused by the increased blood flow to the pelvic area which in turn softens and relaxes the tissues and ligaments in preparation for labour. This means they become more flexible and so are more easily strained, particularly as your centre of gravity has altered thanks to the extra weight you are now carrying. The intestinal muscles also become more relaxed, which can cause complaints such as heartburn (the relaxation of the sphincter muscles at the top of the stomach allows a backflow of acid), and constipation, due to fewer bowel movements. You may find that you need to pass water more often because your baby is pressing down on your bladder. And as your body holds more water when you're pregnant, your fingers, ankles and feet could become swollen, especially if you've been standing for a long time or you are hot. Regular meditation can help to alleviate all these complaints.

How to practise this meditation

As you get bigger, you may find it difficult to sit comfortably in one position for any length of time. Don't prevent yourself from shifting as the discomfort could become distracting, but when you do move, try to change positions with the minimum of effort, making sure you have plenty of support and cushions. To help you immediately refocus, concentrate on your breath and use the same hand position every time as a 'memory cue' to draw you back to where you left off. A common hand position for meditation is with the thumb and forefinger of each hand lightly touching and the other fingers either extended or curled; alternatively, rest your hands on your knees, with your palms turned upwards.

Now use a bodyscan technique to focus your mind on the problem areas. Once you are comfortable and breathing slowly, concentrate on the area of your body you wish to help. For instance, if you are suffering from backache, focus on your back, moving to each point which hurts or feels tense, such as your shoulders or lower back. At each point, as you concentrate on your breaths, imagine the trouble spot feeling flexible, strong and healthy. Spend five to ten breaths on each area, sensing the aches and tension fall away as you do. If you can't pinpoint exactly where the pain is coming from, just visualise your back as a whole. Be aware of particular times or situations when you tend to become strained, and mentally remind yourself to use this bodyscan technique to minimise any problems.

PREVENTING PHYSICAL PROBLEMS

There are a number of practical steps you can take to avoid or alleviate the common physical complaints of the second trimester:

- Backache. Avoid lifting or carrying heavy objects, and try to wear flat shoes. The Alexander technique can help with your posture and osteopathy or chiropractic can help reduce back pains.
- Weak bladder. Rocking backwards and forwards on the toilet helps to reduce pressure on the bladder so that it can be completely emptied. Cut out late evening drinks if you often get up during the night.
- Heartburn. Have frequent small meals, so the stomach doesn't become overfull. Drinking milk can also help to neutralise stomach acid.

- Constipation. Eat plenty of fibre, found in fruit, vegetables, wholemeal bread and bran, and be sure to drink lots of water.
- Water retention. Avoid standing for too long, wear comfortable shoes and put your feet up as often as possible. Regularly rotating each foot one way and then the other can help prevent swelling.

Preparing for antenatal tests

Use this meditation when you want to:
- ◆ *Face anxieties about your baby's wellbeing*
- ◆ *Master fears about having antenatal tests*
- ◆ *Keep the jitters at bay when you're waiting for test results*

You are probably feeling more at ease now that your pregnancy is well established and the uncertainty of the first twelve weeks is over. It is around this time, during the second trimester, that you will have antenatal tests to ensure that you are in good health and that all is progressing well with your baby's development. Several different tests are available. Although most are non-invasive, a few do carry small risks (*see box opposite*), so you need to discuss the necessity of each test with your doctor.

Most pregnancies are perfectly normal, but having tests can be stressful, particularly if you feel you may have cause for concern, perhaps because of your age or family medical history. In turn, this stress can affect your wellbeing and although your baby won't be unduly affected by short-term stress, he or she will be aware of the tension in your body.

Think positively

If you find yourself lying awake at night, worrying about undergoing your antenatal tests, try to look at them as positive procedures which are aimed at helping you and your baby to have a healthy and successful pregnancy.

How to practise this meditation

It can be useful to combine both a full meditation and a 'mini' one on the days when you have a test. This way you can calm and prepare yourself before you set off, then practise a simple technique on the way to the clinic, in the waiting room, or even during a scan to encourage positive thoughts and give you continuous inner balance and tranquillity. For both, focus first on your breathing. Notice how it begins naturally to slow down and regulate as each breath exhales from your body. Count each out-breath, say up to ten before starting again, to keep you focused. For your main meditation,

UNDERSTANDING YOUR ANTENATAL TESTS

You and your baby will be monitored regularly throughout pregnancy. Routine tests include taking your blood pressure to check for signs of pre-eclampsia or hypertension (also characterised by swollen feet and hands and the presence of protein in the urine); urine samples to check for signs of urinary infection or the onset of diabetes (which can temporarily occur during pregnancy) and blood tests to check for anaemia.

Screening tests can give an indication of problems, such as spina bifida, but are not definitive. They include:

✦ Nuchal scan (10–14 weeks). An ultrasound scan to measure the amount of fluid in the back of the baby's neck, which can indicate Down's syndrome.

✦ Double (15–22 weeks) and triple (13–23 weeks) tests are blood tests that analyse two or three hormone levels indicative of Down's syndrome or neural tube defects.

If there is cause for concern after a screening test, you may be offered:

✦ CVS (chorionic villus sampling, 10–12 weeks). A tissue sample is taken from the placenta and analysed for Down's syndrome, chromosome disorders and inherited conditions.

✦ Amniocentesis (14–18 weeks). A sample of fluid is withdrawn from the amniotic sac to detect Down's syndrome, chromosome disorders, inherited conditions and neural defects.

Both of these tests give a definitive result, but carry a slight risk of miscarriage.

---

continue this breathing for fifteen minutes, with both hands placed flat on your tummy so that you feel in touch with your baby. You may also choose a mantra, using a particular word that conveys the positive feelings you have about yourself and your baby. You could choose a word such as 'Calm' or 'Love', or the traditional Hindu mantra, 'Om'.

Mini meditation: to relieve anxiety

Start the mini meditation in the same way. Next, once your breathing has calmed down, think about your bump. Look at it a couple a times and sense its firm roundness. Let your surroundings fade into the background and feel time slow down. Allow your body to relax and your shoulders to drop. Imagine how your bump would feel now if you were gently stroking it – the sensation of your hand on your smooth, bare skin. Then gently bring yourself back into the present and be aware of how calm you are now feeling.

Knowing the sex of your baby

Use this meditation when you want to:

◆ *Make up your mind about whether or not to find out the sex of your child*

◆ *Accept and give thanks for your baby boy or girl, if you do know the sex*

◆ *Welcome the unique individual inside you*

The question of whether or not to find out the sex of the unborn child crosses the mind of most expectant mothers. Some women want to know as soon as possible so that they can prepare themselves, while others want the surprise at the end of labour.

There are many things to consider before deciding to find out the sex of your baby. It's important to discuss these with your partner as he may not wish to know. Will you be disappointed if it's not the sex you were hoping for, and do you think this may affect the rest of your pregnancy? If you do find out, will you tell family and friends? Even if you want to know, people close to you may still want the surprise. Will you feel that now you know, labour may be more of a trial because you don't have the excitement of finding out what you've produced at the end?

But there are also a lot of good reasons for knowing. You will have time to prepare yourself mentally for the arrival of your new son or daughter. This can lead to a closer attachment with your baby before the birth – you'll be able to say 'she's kicking now' or 'he's got hiccups'. You will know how to decorate the nursery and what colours to buy for the baby's layette.

Sometimes it is medically important to know a baby's sex, for example if one or both parents carry a hereditary sex-linked disorder such as haemophilia (a condition in which the blood does not clot properly, leading to profuse bleeding), which usually affects boys only. Ultrasound scans can give a good indication of a baby's sex if the picture is clear, but this isn't always possible to achieve. Alternatively, diagnostic tests (*see page 73*) can give an accurate verdict.

How to practise this meditation

For both the following meditations, once you are comfortable and relaxed, allow thoughts to float into your mind and, rather than trying to dismiss them as you might usually do, focus on them, without censorship, before letting them go. In this way, the constant in-flow and out-flow of thoughts will gradually guide you, allowing you to relax and accept what is in your subconscious mind.

Deciding whether or not to find out the sex of your baby...

Once your breathing is deep and controlled, allow any thoughts concerning your baby to enter your mind. Concentrate on the thought for a second or two, acknowledge it and then let it go, returning to your breathing. Even if it is a thought with which you are not comfortable, such as 'Will I be disappointed if it's a boy?', let it hold your attention but don't try to analyse it, then let it go. As each thought enters and leaves, you will gain greater insight and the decision will eventually come naturally.

If you already know the sex of your baby...

Once you have focused on your breathing and it has become regular, let your mind wander, allowing any thoughts about your baby to enter your consciousness. Repeat whichever word springs up, such as 'girl', 'boy', 'happy', 'close' and so on. Don't analyse your thoughts, just accept them and let them go. By doing this, you will be gaining inner peace and a closeness with your baby.

Bonding with your baby

Use this meditation when you want to:
◆ *Feel close to your baby*
◆ *Tune in to your baby's movements*
◆ *Let your baby know how much love you have to give*

Being aware of your unborn baby is the first step to bonding, creating a closeness that will last you a lifetime. It will also help you adjust to the idea of parenthood, and help make your pregnancy a more rewarding one.

Your baby is not, as was once thought, a foetus without a personality or feelings whose senses only awaken once born. On the contrary, studies have indicated that babies are aware of and can react to stimuli from outside the uterus long before birth. From the first few weeks after conception your baby could brush the inside of your uterus and by now can consciously move in response to external stimuli, such as the stroke of your hand. By sixteen weeks, the ears have developed enough for sounds to be heard — your reassuring heartbeat, the sound of your voice and the rumblings of your stomach — and by twenty-four weeks more distant sounds such as music and your partner's voice can be heard. At the end of this trimester, the eyelids will have separated and your baby will be able to make out changes in brightness for the first time, shying away if a light is too fierce.

> *Love has only a beginning;*
> *It has no end.*
> SANT DARSHAN SINGH

Your baby will be very much in tune with your own feelings from the second trimester of pregnancy onward. When you experience different emotions, chemicals are released into your bloodstream and cross the placenta to your baby — excitement and laughter release endorphins, for example, which help your body respond to stress and will also give your baby that 'feelgood' factor, too; while anger or stress releases adrenaline (*see overleaf*) and will thus make your body feel tense to your baby.

WAYS TO COMMUNICATE WITH YOUR UNBORN BABY

By being aware of your baby, you can tune in to his or her likes and dislikes. For instance, notice if your baby moves more when you play a certain piece of music, or whether his or her activity increases when you are relaxing in a warm bath, the water gently swaying and washing over you. Here are some practical tips for getting close to that little person inside you.

• Touch and stroke your baby as often as possible. The movement and warmth of your hand is very reassuring.

• Talk and sing aloud to your baby. Experiments have shown that, once born, babies can recognise words and music they heard when they were in the uterus.

• Try to direct your thoughts towards your baby. Think positively, say what you feel, explore your expectations and don't worry about the odd negative thought – it won't have an adverse effect.

• Your baby will respond to your movements, being lulled by gentle swaying or walking, and becoming agitated if you are dashing around. So keep your actions relaxed and calm.

How to practise this meditation

This technique involves playing different types of music to see whether you get a response from your baby. Some mothers have found their babies respond to the eerie high and low frequencies of whale and dolphin sounds; others have found vocal or choral music most effective (probably because this is closest in pitch and tone to the mother's voice).

Sit or lie in any position that feels comfortable. As you let the music wash over you, concentrate on your breathing, still your mind and let your body relax. Be aware that your baby can not only hear the music but will also sense the slowing down of your own actions and the tension leaving you. You may want to visualise your baby lying in the uterus, cradled in the warm fluid of the amniotic sac and being soothed by the peace surrounding you. Or you could chant a mantra, so that the sounds reverberate through your body to your baby: choose a word that encapsulates the closeness you feel to your unborn child.

Reducing your stress levels

Use this meditation when you want to:
◆ *Stop feeling pressured by the burdens of your life*
◆ *Slow down, because you're worried stress may be affecting your baby*
◆ *Deal with anxiety about a particular aspect of your pregnancy*

Pregnancy is a wonderfully exciting time, but like any other period in your life, you're also susceptible to stress. And as your hormones play havoc with your emotions, it's not surprising you may sometimes find you're not dealing with certain situations as easily as usual.

As we've seen on pages 78–79, your baby's senses are all being stimulated through you. And although short bursts of anger or stress will do your baby no harm at all, research shows that longer exposure to negative emotions and high stress levels can have an adverse effect. This may lead to a difficult labour, low birthweight or a restless and discontented baby. Happily, however, research also shows that a positive attitude towards your pregnancy and baby means even prolonged stress will have far less impact, as if 'cocooning' your baby.

There are a number of ways of reducing stress. For example, cut down on your workload, if this is what is affecting you, by delegating more. Socialise less if you are not getting enough sleep. Try to stop arguments before they escalate, perhaps by saying aloud 'This isn't good for the baby!' Take more time for yourself just to sit and relax and, at times, do nothing but think about your baby.

How to practise this meditation

Regular meditation can give you a sense of inner peace and tranquillity so the things that used to cause you anxiety, stress you no longer. Begin by concentrating on your breathing, feeling your body and mind slowing down as you count each out-breath. Use visualisation to imagine yourself as the calm, controlled person you would like to be.

◆ *See yourself in any situation in which you are likely to become stressed. Picture how you would like to deal with that situation, how calm you are, how in control. As you come out of your meditation, keep that image with you, so that the next time you are aware of becoming stressed, it will immediately spring to mind.*

Mini meditation: allow yourself to slow down

If you are feeling particularly tense but can't find the time or privacy to meditate alone for a while, this is a very good temporary stress-buster. Start to be aware of each movement you make. Notice how your body feels, how quick and jerky your actions are, think how you may be hurrying to fit more and more things into an already stressful day.

Then carry on your tasks, but make a concerted effort to do them more slowly. Give yourself time to make each conscious movement. Watch your hands as they type or write or go about your daily chores. Slow your voice down, however much in a hurry you are, when you are speaking. Remember: saving seconds will ultimately succeed only in adding minutes of stress to your life. As your movements ease up, let the thoughts rushing through your head slow down too. Start this again each time you begin to feel tense.

THE BENEFITS OF ANTENATAL CLASSES

If you haven't done so already, book your antenatal classes. They are much more than just a 'coffee morning with the girls'. They should cover all aspects of pregnancy, your choices of pain relief during labour, tips on breastfeeding and how to cope with a new-born. They also offer the opportunity to talk about your pregnancy and baby as much as you want without fear of sending others to sleep! Encourage your partner to accompany you, too. This will help him understand what you will be going through, encourage you to practise your breathing and other exercises at home and teach him how to support you during labour.

Loving your changing body

Use this meditation when you want to:

◆ *Overcome the feeling that your body is no longer your own*

◆ *Banish fears that you're putting on too much weight (or that you won't be able to lose it once the baby is born)*

◆ *Rediscover confidence in your attractiveness and sexuality*

During the months of pregnancy, your changing body shape is beautiful evidence of the life growing within you. Alterations that were subtle in the early stages are by now an obvious testament to your unborn child: a thickened waistline, stretched abdomen and breasts heavy in readiness for feeding. But these exciting signs that your body is preparing itself for motherhood can also be difficult to get used to.

If you find you are enjoying the growth of your baby while being uncomfortable with your unfamiliar shape, don't despair. It's perfectly alright to have these feelings: almost every expectant mother does. In fact, negative thoughts are often due to social conditioning – pregnancy means fat means ugly. Yet in many cultures, pregnant women are revered and their bodies thought of as beautiful. Accept that negative thoughts may arise, but understand that you can let these thoughts go while maintaining positive beliefs and visions about your changing shape. Affirmations and visualisations will help you do this: both are powerful tools that can help you turn negative into positive.

Pamper yourself

Add 6–12 drops of an essential oil such as frankincense, known for its meditative properties, to the bath or a vaporiser. (If you are performing this exercise in the first three months of your pregnancy, you must avoid using frankincense. Try using lavender oil instead.)

How to practise this meditation

At this stage of your pregnancy, it may be easier to lie down while you meditate. Choose somewhere quiet and comfortable and, if you are lying on your side, make sure you have a pillow or cushion between your legs to give you proper support. If it's a nice day, lie near an open window so any bird song can be incorporated into your visualisation (*see below*). Alternatively, lie in a warm bath, with your head supported by a rolled towel and the room lit only by a candle.

The following affirmations, when repeated over and over, will help you see your changing body in a very positive light. You could concentrate on particular aspects of your shape or changes to your body. Personalise them to suit your individual needs if you like.

> * *My body is beautiful. It is a growing sign of life within me and is the giver of life.*
> * *I am proud of my body. It is beautiful to the eye and sensual to the touch.*
> * *I accept what comes up in my thoughts and feelings and am learning to love myself for all of me and for the way I am.*

Your transforming body is in itself a very visual image. If you see yourself as beautiful and are proud of your body, others will share in your positive self-image, but if you think of yourself as ungainly and unattractive, then that's what you will be. Create an image along the lines of one of the following, again personalising it to suit your own needs. The clearer the image, the better the results. Repeat it as often as necessary so the image truly becomes a part of you.

- *Imagine yourself running easily and freely along a beautiful seashore. You are moving gracefully, in light clothing. You feel the wind in your hair and the sand beneath your feet; you feel as light as a feather and you can turn and twist as much as you wish.*
- *Imagine being relaxed and at ease with yourself. It is a beautiful day and you are walking confidently along a street, proud of your shape, which shows your fertility and enhances your sense of being a woman. You are aware of admiring glances appreciating your body, but have no need to acknowledge them.*

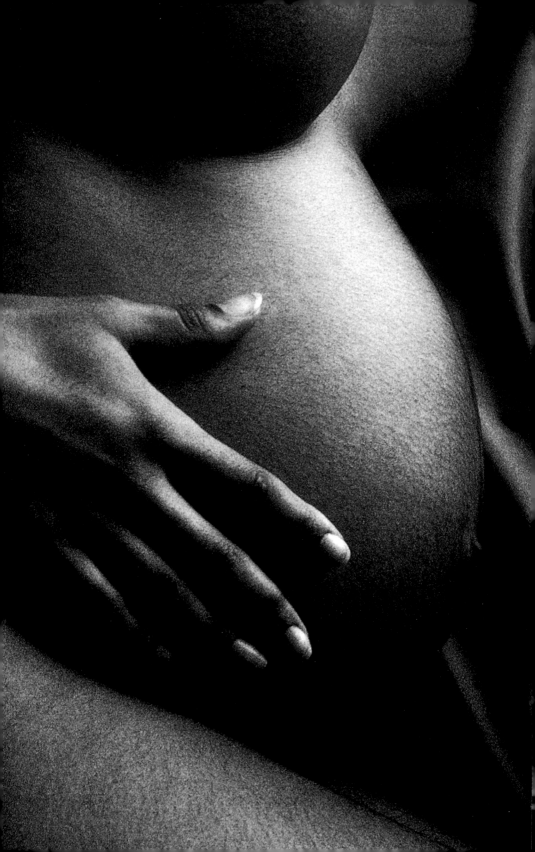

The
third
trimester

You may feel like your pregnancy has been going on forever, but now that you're in the third trimester, an end to the long months of waiting is in sight and it won't be long before you'll have the thrilling experience of holding your baby at last. The larger you get during these weeks, the more difficult it will become to carry out tasks you found simple earlier in your pregnancy, such as shopping, cleaning the house, even getting out of the bath! You will tire more easily, so take things easy, napping when you can. The meditations in this section are aimed at helping you to relax and cope with any problems or anxieties that occur as you near your labour, so you're well prepared for the incredible event of the birth of your child.

Getting a good night's sleep

Use this meditation when you want to:

◆ *Wind down after a tiring day*
◆ *Get to sleep, despite physical discomfort*
◆ *Put an end to wakeful hours of worrying*

Now that you are in your third trimester, you are probably finding it difficult to get a full night's uninterrupted sleep. As your abdomen gets larger, finding a satisfactory position becomes harder. Sleeping on your back may be uncomfortable as the baby is lying against your spine, which can cause tingling, dizziness and breathlessness, while lying on your side means the baby can use you as a 'springboard', pushing against the mattress. Night sweats and frequent trips to the bathroom can also disturb deep sleep. What's more, although *you* may be ready for sleep at night, your *baby* may be on a different timetable and could happily move all night long. You may find that the nearer you get to your due date, night-time becomes a prime time for worried thoughts about the prospect of labour, making it difficult to fall asleep. But the deep sleep you get at night is very important, particularly during the last three months of pregnancy, as this is when your energy is restored.

> *Through sleep and darkness safely*
>   *brought*
> *Restored to life, and power, and thought.*
> JOHN KEBLE

How to practise this meditation

Concentrating on your breathing is one of the best ways to get to sleep. The deeply relaxed state that this type of meditation brings can help slow down your mind and body if you are having difficulty dropping off, and

ROUTES TO BETTER SLEEP

For a more peaceful night, try one or more of the following tips:

• Keep late-night drinks to a minimum, choose decaffeinated tea or coffee and eat a light evening meal to prevent indigestion and heartburn.

• Have a relaxing bath before bed. Add a couple of drops of an essential oil to the water, such as camomile, which relieves stress and tension.

• Ensure your bedroom is conducive to sleep (dark and not too warm), the phone is switched off and your bed is giving you proper support.

• Support your legs or back with a cushion or pillow.

• Avoid reading about labour just before switching off the lights   stick to a book that won't get your thoughts churning!

• Keep daytime naps to the morning or early afternoon so that they don't interrupt your nocturnal sleep patterns.

focus your mind on getting back to sleep if you have woken. Before you begin, support your back or legs (if lying on your side) with a cushion or pillow to make you more comfortable. Now, close your eyes and, starting from the top of your head, visually work your way down your body, imagining any tension easing away. Focus on your breathing, counting each breath as you exhale, up to ten, then repeat. Alternatively, silently say 'Sleep' each time you breathe out. Don't worry about how quickly or slowly you are breathing.

When your mind wanders, acknowledge any thoughts, but let them go and return your attention to your breathing. Although the less you move around the easier it is to concentrate, don't feel you can't shift at all as the wish to change positions will become distracting. When you need to move, do so slowly until you are comfortable, without losing count of your breaths. As you feel yourself becoming more and more relaxed, stop counting and focus only on your breathing.

Looking ahead to motherhood

Use this meditation when you want to:

✦ *Prepare yourself for the long-term (motherhood) and not just for
the immediate future (labour)*
✦ *Examine your expectations about what lies ahead*
✦ *Reassure yourself you will retain your self-identity*

These last few weeks are among the most exciting time of your pregnancy,
and the days can now appear frustratingly long as you impatiently wait for
the new arrival. The excitement is also often tinged with anxiety about
labour and how you will cope with life beyond labour: the hard – but
fulfilling – job of looking after a baby. It's natural to have some worries
about how your life is going to change and how you will adapt, but being
aware that your life *will* change is the first step to an exciting new life.

No one can give you any guarantees, but the fact that most women
have more than one child is a good indicator that labour and motherhood
is obviously worthwhile! What mothers, midwives and doctors all agree
on is that the more prepared you are, the more easily you will cope. It's
important to feel relaxed and calm during the last few weeks. It is now
that you need to focus on yourself and your own needs. If you haven't
stopped work already, you should soon be on maternity leave which will
leave you more time to yourself. Meditation can help you to relax, focus
on your needs and calm any worries you may have. If you feel peaceful and
at ease, then so will your baby who can benefit from your relaxed pace,
tranquil thoughts and easy-going attitude.

How to practise this meditation
This technique will help to focus your thoughts so that when the future
become reality, you will be better prepared to deal with any situation
calmly and positively.

ALTERNATIVE WAYS TO RELAX

If you are prone to anxiety, you may like to explore an alternative remedy to help you beat stress. The aim of many natural therapies is to improve the wellbeing of the whole body, not just treat a specific symptom, although each works in a slightly different way. Try one or several of the following, but do consult the advice of a qualified practitioner first.

✦ Homeopathy treats the whole person – mentally, physically and emotionally – rather than just the symptoms. It works by helping the body to heal itself on the basis of treating like with like. Small amounts of the treatment, that would in larger doses cause the complaint, actually ease it. Remedies are given in different potencies, usually in pilules.

✦ Herbal remedies use the healing properties of plants, trees, flowers and herbs. A mixture of herbs are taken in the form of a tea, infusion, decoction or added to a bath.

✦ Flower remedies are said to contain the 'energy' imprint of a plant which works on the vibrations of our own energy patterns, restoring the flow disrupted, for instance, by anxiety. The essences are dropped onto the tongue or taken in water.

✦ Aromatherapy uses the aromatic oil essences of plants and flowers, diluted in a carrier oil, to heal mentally and physically. These can be inhaled if added to a bath or vaporiser, or absorbed through the skin during massage. Always make sure that the oil you use is suitable during pregnancy.

✦ Reflexology is based on the principle that each part of the foot corresponds to an area of the body and that massaging certain points on the foot can relieve physical problems.

Start by picking an object that is beautiful to you – a vase of flowers, the flame of a candle, a tree in the garden – and sit or lie in front of it. As you focus on each out-breath, you will be aware of noises around you – a neighbour talking, a car starting, or somebody's radio – but just acknowledge these are present, don't let them distract you.

Observe the details of what you are looking at: the texture of a petal, the way the flame dances in movement, the rustle of leaves as the tree sways in the wind. Silently name what you are seeing with each out-breath (for instance, petal). Repeat a few times and then move on to another aspect (e.g. blue) and then another (say, moving), until you feel as if you are becoming part of what you are looking at, part of the beauty. Slowly come out of the meditation and be aware of how your mind has focused and how relaxed your body feels.

Preparing yourself for labour

Use this meditation when you want to:

◆ *Feel empowered about the impending birth*
◆ *Quell your nerves about what labour will be like*
◆ *Remind yourself that your beautiful baby will make all the waiting and discomfort worthwhile*

Your pregnancy and labour together comprise a very personal and unique period in your life – yet many women tend to feel anxious as they feel they are not in control. Fears about being unable to cope with the pain, having an epidural or not being allowed to move around can justifiably gain great significance. But, within the confines of safety, you should be able to do what you want during your labour. Help yourself by being prepared. Together with your partner, read up about all the options available to you and decide on a birth plan that you feel happy with. Don't be pressured into making any decisions you're not sure about – be assertive about what you want. Talk to your midwife or consultant well before your due date and explain what you would like. If you're having your baby in hospital, visit the delivery room, find out about the hospital's policy on giving epidurals and what the rate is for Caesarean sections. And remember that the medical staff at hospital are there to make sure the delivery is as safe and supportive as possible for both you and the baby.

What worked for me

The nearer I got to my due date, the more anxious I seemed to become about the impending labour. I decided to sit down every day for a few minutes to analyse what my concerns were and to try to work out what I would want to happen if they actually arose. Just sorting my feelings out in my own mind made me feel more in control.

Being in control is not only about knowing what you want, but also acknowledging that this may have to change if things don't go according to plan. No birth is perfect, so the more open-minded you and your partner are about the way the birth might go, the more you will be able to cope if things don't work out the way you wished.

How to practise this meditation

Pick an affirmation that summarises how you would like to feel, such as:

★ *I am in control*
★ *I want what is best for my baby*
★ *What is good for my baby is good for me*
★ *My mind and body are calm.*

Then sit or lie down, making yourself as comfortable as possible. Focus on your breathing, becoming aware of how it slows and regulates, and silently repeat your affirmation. If you do this daily, your affirmation will become part of your subconscious and enter your conscious mind when needed.

Mini meditation: being aware of your senses

Use the following meditation for a minute or two when you begin to feel overwhelmed by fears – at the kitchen sink, in the car, as you lie in the bath. Begin by focusing on what's happening around you. For instance, as you lie in the bath, notice the sensation of the water moving against your body, its heat, your toes pressed against the end of the bath. Don't stop whatever you're doing, just be aware that you are doing it. You could concentrate on one sense, silently repeating the word 'Touch' or 'Sound'. This draws you away from unproductive worries and calms you down.

CALMING AIDS IN HOSPITAL

You should prepare a bag with all the essentials you and your newborn will need in hospital about three weeks before your due date. You may also like to consider packing a few things to take into the delivery room, to help you through labour, such as:

• A favourite small ornament to focus on
• Calming music that you have used before
• Comfortable cushions for support
• An aromatherapy scented handkerchief
• An atomiser water spray to freshen your face
• A flannel or sponge to cool you down

• A book or magazine to take your mind off labour if your contractions slow down
• Biscuits to keep you going
• Extra cushions to prop you up

Preparing your baby for birth

Use this meditation when you want to:

◆ *Communicate with your baby*

◆ *Stimulate your child for the journey that lies ahead*

◆ *Ready your baby for life outside the uterus*

As your abdomen enlarges and the long-awaited birth of your baby is soon to become a reality, the bond between you both is strengthening. While you are mentally and physically preparing yourself, so too is your baby. At about thirty-six weeks, the baby's head usually engages or drops down into the pelvis in readiness for birth (although this may not happen until a bit later), and all five of the infant's senses are perfectly developed in preparation for life in the outside world.

Babies cry when they're unhappy or want something, so it's not surprising most cry in protest at birth. But some women say so strong was the bond formed in the uterus that their baby made no whimper, only gazing intently up at mother.

Even after a straightforward delivery, it will be a shock for your baby to leave the warm, dark, watery environment of your uterus and enter a bright hospital room, full of strange people. And a more difficult birth – involving ventouse, forceps or a Caesarean delivery, for example – will be even more traumatic. Although there is only a limited amount you can do truly to prepare your baby for the arduous voyage through the birth canal, the more calm, relaxed and prepared you both feel, the more easily you will both cope with the actual birth. Use the following exercise as a means of communication in the run-up to your due-date, letting positive thoughts of peace and tranquillity flow through your body and envelop your baby.

How to practise this meditation

You can use this not only as a daily meditation, when you are sitting or lying down, but also as a mini meditation, to be incorporated into your day as and when you have a spare minute or so. Begin by focusing on your breathing. As you start to breathe more deeply, imagine each inhalation passing down from your nose to your baby, carrying energising oxygen for the journey ahead. Feel your mind begin to calm down with each out-breath and notice your body begin to relax, the tension ebb out from your joints and muscles and feel your limbs loosen. Now repeat one of the following affirmations out loud:

* *Mummy loves you*
* *All is well*
* *We two are one*

Alternatively, you can repeat a mantra, choosing a sound that conveys all you want for a positive delivery for both you and your baby. If you perform this meditation often enough in your last trimester, your unborn baby will begin to recognise the words, so you can use the same affirmation or mantra when you first hold your baby in your arms – this will be very comforting to him or her.

BEST ENVIRONMENT FOR BIRTH

You can ease your baby's transition into the outside world by making the delivery room a peaceful (at least, as far as is possible) and almost familiar place.

✦ Ask to have the lights turned as low as possible during the last stages of labour.

✦ Try to sit up, squat or lean up against your partner during labour, as gravity will help your baby to be delivered naturally.

✦ Play a soothing piece of music during labour, which you have been regularly listening to during your pregnancy – a familiar sound for your baby.

✦ Consider a water birth. Talk to your midwife about facilities at your hospital.

✦ Ask for your baby to be put against your breast immediately so that he or she can feel your warmth and start suckling.

Positive pain relief

Use this meditation when you want to:
+ *Practise controlling your breathing in preparation for labour*
+ *Cope as effectively as possible with pain during delivery*

If you're feeling apprehensive about how you'll cope during labour, don't worry, you're not alone. Every pregnant woman has the same fears and yet, one way or another, we all get through it and are usually prepared to endure it again! No pain is pleasant, but consider labour pain as a 'positive pain' – you know there is a beginning and an end, after which you will have your beautiful, longed-for baby.

Although there is no way of gauging how intense your contractions will be or how you will manage with the pain, your attitude can help you enormously. Fear and anxiety will make you more tense and less able to cope, whereas the more in control and calm you feel, the more you will be able to 'ride' with the pain. Learn about the different methods of pain relief available to you, such as TENS, gas and air, pethidine or epidural (*see opposite*). Be open-minded about what you might need and don't put yourself through pain unnecessarily: it will leave you more exhausted, just at the time when you'll need all your energy to care for your new baby.

How to practise this meditation
You will find that the breathing techniques and ways of focusing your mind used during meditation will be helpful in keeping you calm and in control during your labour. As each contraction builds up, feeling like a tight band around your abdomen, concentrate on your breathing, taking deep breaths and keeping it slow and controlled. It will help if you can focus on

an object in the room — something you've brought that you have used as a calming visual aid in the past, or even just the end of the bed. As the contraction begins to fade, consciously relax your shoulders and let your body relax in preparation for the next one. Silently repeat a mantra or affirmation which will help to give you confidence to keep going, such as:

* *One contraction more is one contraction less*
* *I am coping*
* *It comes, it goes*
* *There is an end*

Remember, the first stage of labour can last many hours, so try to pace yourself. While you're still at home, take things easy, carrying out this meditation while preparing for hospital or, if you're having a home birth, waiting for the midwife to arrive.

As labour progresses, keep in mind all the things you've learned over the past few months to prepare you for this wonderful event. Focus your mind, use your partner for emotional and physical support, and find the position in which you feel most comfortable.

ALTERNATIVE PAIN RELIEF DURING LABOUR

If you would like to have a natural birth but worry that you will be unable to cope with the pain of labour, try one of the methods of pain management discussed below, as well as the breathing technique described in the main meditation. None of these remedies will have any side effects on you or your baby.

✦ Birthing pools. Even if you don't want to give birth in the pool, sitting immersed in warm, soothing water can bring relief during contractions. Ask if your hospital has one; if not, they can be hired.

✦ Hypnosis. Sessions during the latter stages of pregnancy can store positive, relieving images in the subconscious mind, which can later be brought to the fore when you need them, helping you through labour.

✦ TENS machines. These send a small electrical current which blocks the pain impulses to the brain and also stimulates the release of endorphins, your body's own natural painkillers. Many hospitals have TENS machines, or they can be hired.

✦ Acupuncture. This can be used at the start of contractions and throughout labour. Fine, sterilised needles are inserted into points along invisible channels or meridians in the body. The Chinese believe that good health depends upon the flow of 'chi' or energy along these channels. Backache during labour, for instance, may occur as a result of a blockage along the meridians The needles are used to release such blockages so that 'chi' energy can flow freely.

The
new
arrival

*C*ongratulations — at last you have your long-awaited baby! The anticipation of the last nine months is over, the daunting prospect of labour has come and gone and now you can concentrate all your energies on your precious infant. Although you are probably feeling exhausted, the excitement of having a new addition to the family and caring for this small, vulnerable being will somehow carry you through the fatigue of the early weeks. But get as much rest as you can and give yourself time to recover by accepting any help offered. Fit in your meditations when you can, if only for a few minutes each day, and use the time to relax and focus on getting your body back to optimum health.

Celebrating the birth

Use this meditation when you want to:

◆ *Welcome the newest member of your family*
◆ *Give thanks for your baby's safe delivery*
◆ *Cope with being overwhelmed by your feelings for your newborn*

Holding your newborn in your arms for the first is a truly amazing and emotional experience. The intense love a mother feels for her child is like no other and is something to be cherished. The bonding process can take longer to set in for some women than for others, but the depth of feeling combined with the awesome responsibility of looking after something so small, needy and vulnerable, hits all new mothers.

Fit in a meditation when you can

Don't feel guilty if you find yourself meditating less because your routine has been turned upside down. Meditate when you can and remember that it is bound to be more difficult to concentrate when you have so much else on your mind. But try to fit in a couple of minutes every day — by occasionally being able to relax, you will also be benefitting your baby.

Don't forget that your emotions — heightened by the physical experience of delivery, the exhaustion that comes with sleepless nights and a demanding baby — will probably be swinging all over the place. Meditating during these early weeks can not only help to centre you but also provide you with a few rare minutes to yourself. Even if you can't closet yourself away physically, you can mentally withdraw to a more peaceful place while you are doing something else, such as breast-feeding or changing your baby's nappy.

How to practise this meditation

For the first few days after the birth of your baby, you will probably find it easier to fit in a few mini meditations, rather than a full fifteen- or twenty-minute session (when you're more likely to fall asleep than keep your mind alert!). Use the time to focus your thoughts and energies, starting off by just becoming aware of your breathing. Focus on the flow of your breath as it enters and leaves your nose, cool on the inhalation and warm on the exhalation. Feel your shoulders relax down and notice how all the tension in your body flows out from your head to your toes.

Next choose a mantra or affirmation which reflects the way you feel. You can either devise your own, or try one of the following:

✴ *We are one*
✴ *Om*
✴ *Love*
✴ *My longed for baby is here*
✴ *I give thanks for my baby*
✴ *Love encompasses all*

Say the mantra or affirmation out loud so that your newborn hears the comforting sound of your voice, and let your baby be the focus for your meditation. However, if you are feeling overwhelmed by emotions for your newborn, you may prefer to spend your precious few minutes of meditation concentrating on something other than your baby. In this case, try focusing on a vase of flowers, a tree or a mandala instead.

See yourself in perfect health

Use this meditation when you want to:
◆ *Get over a long or difficult birth*
◆ *Heal more quickly, whether your labour was straightforward or you had a Caesarean delivery*
◆ *Overcome feelings of exhaustion*

As every new mother knows, the joy of having a newborn baby is accompanied by exhaustion and discomfort after giving birth. But while the lack of sleep, fatigue and soreness have to take second place to the demands of your baby, it's important to rest as much as possible and to try and relax.

There are a number of problems that can affect you after the birth. The withdrawal of pregnancy hormones once your baby is born will leave you feeling tired until your body has had time to readjust. A tear or episiotomy (cut) in the perineum necessitating stitches, or the appearance of piles, caused by strain on the pelvic floor veins during labour, can be painful and make it difficult to sit comfortably. You may also feel cramps as your uterus contracts to its pre-pregnancy size. If you have had a Caesarean, your abdominal scar will be sore to begin with, but should heal within three weeks.

You don't want any discomfort to take priority over being able to happily enjoy your baby, so use the following meditation to relax you, body and mind. Research shows that meditating can decrease the distress associated with pain, making it easier to bear. The less your discomfort controls your moods and actions, the more quickly you will heal.

How to practise this meditation
Try to find a position that is comfortable for you, if only for a few minutes at a time. Focus on your breathing, being aware of each out-breath as it becomes slower and more regulated. Shake your body to release any ten-

sion and loosen your jaw, so that your teeth are not clenched together. Start to scan your body, beginning at the top of your head. Align your head with your neck and back, drop your shoulders and each time you breathe out, sense that you are exhaling Your tension. Carry on doing this as you mentally and physically feel release as you move down your body.

As an alternative to the body scan, choose a piece of music that lifts your spirits and fosters a feeling of wellbeing. Ideally it could be something that is enjoyable for your baby to listen to, sending him or her off to sleep. If played regularly, your baby will soon associate this time with napping, leaving you in peace to concentrate on yourself. Once your baby is asleep, sit or lie in a comfortable position and just let yourself tune into the melody. Try to imagine what the composer was attempting to evoke when writing the music and let yourself gently move to its rhythm. Let the postive vibrations course through your body, as if each reverberation is shattering areas of discomfort and pain, leaving you with a feeling of energy and revitalisation.

> *SNACK WHEN YOU CAN*
>
> A healthy snack, such as pitta bread and houmous, a slice of quiche or a sandwich will help keep up your energy levels. Keeping nourished means your immune system will be more efficient, leaving you less vulnerable to illness and enabling your body to heal quicker.

You are a good mother

Use this meditation when you want to:

✦ Reconcile your expectations of motherhood with the reality
✦ Reassure yourself that you are doing the best for your baby
✦ Believe in yourself as a mother
✦ Pamper yourself for a change

Until you have experienced parenthood for yourself, you cannot understand the pure joy of holding your own baby in your arms. But the reality of the first few weeks of motherhood can be very different from what you expected. A live and kicking baby who constantly cries and demands feeding and changing may not be the perfect image of the sweet little bundle, cradled in your arms, which you dreamed of when you were pregnant. You may also find it is taking time for you to bond with your baby. Your infant may be fractious, perhaps difficult to console because of colic.

> Take time for yourself, think well of yourself, make peace with yourself and get in touch with yourself
>
> RUTH FISHEL

Feelings of inadequacy – that you are not doing it right, that you don't have the patience needed, that you are somehow failing – are very common among new mothers. You are not alone. As one mother-and-baby expert says, no first-time mother has the instant knowledge of how perfectly to look after her baby. It takes time to adjust, to learn.

It can be easy to believe you are not being a good mother when you feel tired, fraught or things are getting on top of you. But you are a good mother. To help you through the difficult first few weeks, you need to look at your own needs so that you can also look after the needs of your baby. Use the following meditation to calm your mind, focus on what's important and let go of everything else.

LOOK AFTER YOURSELF

It is not easy to look after your baby if you are not looking after yourself. Make sure you have enough provisions for you and the baby – for example, you will feel more in control when you give your newborn a bath if you ensure you have everything within easy reach; and be sure to keep your supply of nappies well stocked too, so you don't have an unnecessary panic.

Other tips for keeping on top of life as a new mother include:

• If you're feeling tired, restrict visitors – they'll understand you need time to rest.

• Be realistic – there is no such thing as a perfect mother. Just be yourself and do your best for your baby.

• Get plenty of rest – nap when you can and accept all offers of help.

• Take time out from time to time – meditate, go for a walk, stare out of the window – anything that is just for yourself.

• Eat well – lots of fresh snacks will keep your energy levels up.

• Don't take on too much – forget the housework, eat simple meals, and turn on the answering machine.

How to practise this meditation

Grab those few precious moments when the baby is asleep, or when you are feeding, as time for yourself. Use music as part of your meditation – a soothing, gentle non-vocal piece – which your baby can enjoy, if awake and feeding, as well as you. Start by becoming aware of your posture and your breathing, making sure you are comfortable. Let the music wash over you, become absorbed by it, aware of each note. Allow whatever images it conjures up to enter your mind and drift away again, but don't let your mind wander   keep bringing it back to the music and how it is making you feel. When the music has finished be aware of how attuned you are to what you were listening to, how you are sitting, breathing and how relaxed you now feel.

Coping with the baby blues

Use this meditation when you want to:

✦ *Stop feelings of panic or depression in their tracks*
✦ *Explore the full range of emotions washing over you*
✦ *Get used to the changes to your body and your life*

Feeling down after the birth of your baby is not an unusual experience. The majority of women suffer from what's called the 'baby blues' to some extent in the first few days or weeks. This is characterised by feeling weepy, irritable, extremely vulnerable, forgetful and prone to quite intense mood swings, experiencing euphoria one moment and over-whelming melancholy the next.

The main cause of the baby blues is thought to be the dramatic drop in the quantity of hormones circulating in the blood following delivery. These hormones rise to high levels during pregnancy, so when they sud-denly plummet within days of giving birth, your body has little chance to adjust, affecting you both mentally and emotionally. Other factors, such as the new feelings of responsibility, tiredness, the change in priorities both you and your partner have to adapt to and any previous problems can all contribute. The blues tend to set in a few days after birth and can last for around ten days. Such emotional swings can be very disorienting if you've never experienced them before, but knowing that they are quite natural and very common may help you through this short-lived period.

More seriously, some mothers suffer from postnatal depression (PND). This may occur within the first four to six weeks after the birth, but may not develop until six months later. Symptoms include a sense of hopelessness, feeling tense, lethargic, panic-stricken and despondent. Sufferers find it difficult to sleep, lose interest in what's going on around them, have obsessional thoughts and find it hard to concentrate. Don't be afraid to seek help if you are suffering from some of these symptoms. You are not just over-reacting to the difficulties of motherhood – PND is a physical illness that affects about one in six new mothers and can be treated. Antidepressants or hormonal treatment can be prescribed, and your health visitor, doctor and family should also give you support. With such help, full recovery usually occurs within weeks.

How to practise this meditation

Using visualisation is more than just conjuring up fantasies: it helps you to focus on whatever is on your mind, to promote positive images, and most importantly, it enables you to relax. (If you drift into daydreaming, however, this is not a true meditation.) The way the visualisation affects you in terms of inducing peace and tranquillity is more important than the image you actually create.

Begin by becoming comfortable and relaxed, your body releasing tension with each out-breath. A simple visualisation is just to concentrate on one thing in particular – an object or a rainbow, for instance. Begin to feel a sense of what you are imagining – the outline, texture, shape, density. Imagine yourself becoming what you are visualising. How does it feel, what sensations are you experiencing? Don't force it, but be aware of whatever comes into your mind naturally. Slowly let the image dissolve and be aware of how you are feeling, how your body and mind are relaxed and focused.

ALTERNATIVE REMEDIES FOR POSTNATAL DEPRESSION

As well as physical and emotional support from family, friends and the medical profession, and getting plenty of rest, complementary therapies have proved useful for many women dealing with postnatal depression. If you are interested in such treatments, consult a qualified practitioner.

✦ Homeopathy. This is believed to work by inducing symptoms similar to those caused by the disease itself, thereby stimulating the body's natural healing mechanisms. Among the remedies thought to help women suffering from PND are: *Natrum mur* for feelings of guilt, withdrawal and irritability; *Pulsatilla* when you can't stop crying; and *Sepia* when you feel tired and irritable, or have no interest in your surroundings.

✦ Naturopathy. A well balanced diet is essential for looking after yourself and your baby. You may be lacking certain vitamins and minerals after pregnancy and a naturopath may advise taking the B vitamins (particularly B6), vitamin C and magnesium, calcium, iron and potassium mineral supplements.

✦ Acupuncture. This form of treatment can help to rebalance your hormone levels which have soared during pregnancy and then dramatically dipped following the birth. It is also thought to help release hormones to combat depression naturally.

Meeting your energy needs

Use this meditation when you want to:
- *Get through the day having been up all night feeding and changing nappies*
- *Overcome your lethargy and exhaustion*

The early days of motherhood can be tiring. Recovering from the birth and attending to your baby's needs day and night can mean your energy levels hit rock bottom. It is difficult to enjoy or feel enthusiastic about anything, even your beautiful new baby, when you feel exhausted, easily irritated and depressed by minor setbacks. Meditation can give your body and mind the rest that you may have been denied through lack of sleep. As well as meditating, try to think positively. Your thoughts are energy and the quality of those thoughts affects your physical energy levels. Keep reminding yourself that this exhausting period will end soon. Your baby will become more settled, you will sleep better, and life with your baby will become more rewarding and much more fun.

> *Meditation is the freeing of energy in abundance.*
> JIDDHU KRISHNAMURTI

How to practise this meditation
Newborn babies sleep for between sixteen and twenty hours a day, so you should be able to find twenty minutes when you can meditate. Any meditation, however simple, can help to restore your energy levels, but you might like to try the following.

Sitting comfortably or lying down, allow yourself to become relaxed and focus on your breathing. Breathe right down into your pelvis and as you do so, see yourself pull in vibrant red light and visualise it spreading throughout your pelvis, around your back and into your buttocks. When you breathe out, see yourself breathing grey fog out of the pelvic area.

Continue to breathe red light into your pelvis until it feels as if all the grey fog has gone and the area feels lighter and more energised. Next, breathe in to your navel and see the breath flow in as orange light that spreads out around your waist. Breathe out grey fog and continue to breathe in orange until your abdomen feels full of radiant orange light. Now focus on the area between your navel and your ribs and breathe yellow light in to fill this area. Focus on your chest area and breathe in green light. Breathe sky blue light into your throat and, bringing your attention to the centre of your forehead, breathe in indigo light. Finally, focus on the crown of your head and breathe soft violet light into this area. When all parts of your body feel full of radiant colour, breathe out pure white light and let it surround you. When you are ready, bring your awareness back to your surroundings and get up slowly.

Take it easy

Traditionally women had a 'lying-in' period after birth, a time when you could be with your baby and be cared for by other women. Nowadays, women think they ought to get back to normal as soon as possible, but try not to demand too much of yourself. Rest or nap when you can, and try to sleep when your baby sleeps. Enlist the help and support of family and friends, forget about cooking and cleaning for a few days and put a Do Not Disturb sign on your bedroom door when you need a rest.

Breathing more efficiently also helps to beat fatigue. Shallow breathing, where you inhale into the chest only, deprives every cell in your body of the oxygen needed for energy. Watch your baby as he or she sleeps and you'll see how it should be done. Babies inhale so deeply that their whole chest and abdominal area rises with every breath. Making a conscious effort to emulate your baby's breathing pattern can improve your energy levels and your general well-being.

When you are breast-feeding

Use this meditation when you want to:
- ✦ *Encourage successful feeding and bonding*
- ✦ *Make breast-feeding as pleasurable as possible*
- ✦ *Stop feeling discouraged in the early stages*

Breast-feeding is the most natural and healthy way to feed your baby. It helps your body return to normal more quickly and provides your baby with all the nutrients he or she needs for rapid development in the early months. Breast milk contains antibodies that make your baby more resistant to infections and less prone to constipation and digestive upsets. The act of feeding also helps you to form a close and loving bond with each other. One of the hormones that stimulates milk flow is also partly responsible for the overwhelming love that a new mother can feel for her baby.

> *When you are in your own intimate place, a place that you have created you realise that when (a woman) breast-feeds an intense flow of energy surges through her whole body.* SHEILA KITZINGER

If you don't feel this immediately, don't worry, just enjoy the wonderful feeling of your baby nuzzling against you and delight in the softness and closeness of this special little person.

Sometimes, breast milk does not flow properly to begin with. Your breasts may become painful or engorged or your baby may have difficulty latching on. All of these are common problems, so try not to get discouraged too early or too easily. With patience, practice and positive thinking every woman is capable of breast-feeding. But, if you really feel it is not for you, try not to feel guilty. Use a good formula milk and make as much time as possible for closeness and intimacy with your baby.

TIPS FOR SUCCESSFUL BREAST-FEEDING

Your breasts can produce enough milk provided they are stimulated to do so. Sucking stimulates milk production and all babies are born with a natural sucking reflex, so put your baby to the breast as soon and as often as possible.

• Gently stroke the cheek nearest the breast to encourage your baby to turn open-mouthed towards the nipple.

• All babies need time to get used to feeding, so be patient, take your lead from your baby and try to feed whenever he or she is hungry.

• Talking or singing can soothe a fretful or distracted feeder.

• Relax: being tense can restrict milk flow so do a meditation or relaxation exercise every day.

How to practise this meditation

This simple balancing meditation can help to relieve tension and normalise body functioning. Begin in the usual way by sitting quietly and focus on your breathing. When you feel relaxed, take a deep breath and chant 'Ong'. Chant aloud and hold the sound for as long as is comfortable, feeling it vibrate in your nose and against the roof of your mouth. Inhale again, slowly and deeply, and repeat 'Ong', chanting at your own pace. Aim to lengthen and deepen your breath with every inhalation without gasping for air. Let yourself become enveloped in the sound of the mantra and feel yourself as a balanced, healthy and productive person. Know that your body can do all that nature intended it to do easily and effortlessly. Encourage these feelings and allow them to grow in place of any negative or unhealthy feelings you may have. Continue to chant and believe in yourself until you feel it's time to bring your meditation to an end.

If you'd like to extend the meditation, or feel an affirmation would help to relax you *during* breast-feeding, one of the following may help to encourage your milk flow:

* *My body is working perfectly*
* *I can meet all my baby's needs*
* *I am happy providing for my baby*

Now you're a family

Use this meditation when you want to:
+ *Bond together as a three- (or more-) some*
+ *Feel happy and relaxed about sharing your baby's care*
+ *Enjoy your new responsibilities*

These early days are not just about bonding with your baby, but about bonding as a family. You may feel that the baby is primarily your responsibility, especially if you are breast-feeding and your partner is at work for most of the day. But it's easy for a new dad to feel left out, so try to think of yourself as part of a family that shares love and responsibility. Be patient with your partner, who may be afraid to hold the baby even though he wants to. He may feel clumsy, afraid that he might drop or somehow 'break' this seemingly fragile little creature. Encourage him to get involved in all aspects of the baby's care as soon and as much as he can, so that he becomes more confident and forms a close attachment with your child early on. If you are breast-feeding, you can express milk into a bottle so that your partner can also become involved with feeding. This should also give you more time to relax and practise your meditation.

Research at the University of Southern California showed that people who meditated were more happily married than other couples. They attributed their happiness to being more relaxed, loving and accepting of each other, while continuing to grow as individuals. Being relaxed parents also means you are more likely to have a relaxed and contented child, as babies pick up on their parents' mood and tend to respond accordingly.

How to practise this meditation

Let your partner look after the baby while you find a quiet spot where you won't be disturbed. Sit comfortably, check your body for tension, breathe deeply and let it go. Take another deep breath and as you breathe out, close your eyes and silently say 'Relax'. Continue to breathe at a pace you find comfortable, without trying to control it and on every out-breath say 'Relax'. Remember to match the affirmation to your breath and not the other way round. After a few minutes, when you feel completely relaxed, introduce the affirmation 'We are one'. Your breath may have slowed down by now, so just let it find its own pace and each time you breathe out say, 'We are one'. Continue to repeat the affirmation on every out-breath. If, after some time, you find it difficult to stay focused on your affirmation, just let it float to the back of your mind and simply turn your attention to your breath, knowing that you can pick up your affirmation again at any time. When you are ready, bring your awareness back to your surroundings, open your eyes and get up slowly.

Remember that you can use an affirmation of your choice to promote bonding at any time during the day, when feeding or changing your baby, for example, in the bath or as you lie down to sleep.

A tender touch

Babies are happiest when their skin is touching yours. Cuddle your baby and have your partner cuddle her when you are naked so she can feel and smell your skin and hear your heart beat. Research has also shown that babies become more alert, happy and sociable and sleep better at night when they are massaged. Try to make time for a regular family massage in the evening. Wait at least half an hour after you have eaten and choose a time when your baby is neither hungry nor just after a feed, and when she seems happy to be stroked. In a warm room, using a little plain vegetable oil, gently massage your baby and each other for a few minutes before bedtime. This is relaxing, bonding and a pleasure for all of you.

USEFUL ADDRESSES

ACTIVE BIRTH CENTRE
113A Chetwynd Road
London, NW5 1DA
Tel: 020 7482 5554

ASSOCIATION OF RADICAL
MIDWIVES
62 Greetby Hill
Ormskirk
Lancashire, L39 2DT
Tel: 01695 572 776

THE BRITISH
CHIROPRACTIC
ASSOCIATION
Blagrave House
17 Blagrave Street
Reading, RG1 1QB
Tel: 0118 950 5950

THE BRITISH
HOMOEOPATHIC
ASSOCIATION
27A Devonshire Street
London, W1N 1RJ
Tel: 020 7935 2163

FERTILITY UK
Clitherow House
1 Blythe Mews
London, W14 0NW
Tel: 020 7371 1341

FORESIGHT
28 The Paddock
Godalming
Surrey, GU7 1XD
Tel: 01483 427 839

FRIENDS OF THE WESTERN
BUDDHIST ORDER
London Buddhist Centre
51 Roman Road
London, E2 0HU
Tel: 020 8981 1225

GINGERBREAD NATIONAL
OFFICE FOR LONE PARENTS
16–17 Clerkenwell Close
London, EC1R 0AN
Tel: 020 7336 8183

INSTITUTE FOR
COMPLEMENTARY MEDICINE
PO Box 194
London, SE16 7QZ
Tel: 020 7237 5165

ISSUE THE NATIONAL
FERTILITY ASSOCIATION
114 Lichfield Street
Walsall
Warwickshire, WS1 1SZ
Tel: 01922 722888

LA LECHE LEAGUE
BMC 3424
London, WC1N 3XX
Tel: 020 7242 1278

MISCARRIAGE ASSOCIATION
c/o Clayton Hospital
Northgate, Wakefield
West Yorkshire, WF1 3JS
Tel: 01924 200799

NATIONAL CHILDBIRTH
TRUST (NCT)
Alexandra House
Oldham Terrace
Acton
London, W3 6NH
Tel: 020 8992 8637

TRANSCENDENTAL
MEDITATION (TM)
National Communications
Office, Beacon House
Willow Walk
Woodley Park
Skelmersdale, WN8 6UR
Tel: 0990 143 733

INDEX

ACKNOWLEDGEMENTS

Illustrators Joanna Logan,
Josephine Sumner

Picture researcher Sandra
Schneider

**Additional editorial
assistance** Dawn Henderson

**Additional design
assistance** Sandra Brooke

Photographic sources
3 and 97 Tony Stone Images
8 Images Colour Library
30 Images Colour Library/
Charles Walker Collection
38 Images Colour Library
50 Tony Stone Images
66 The Stock Market
73 Tony Stone Images
77 Bubbles/Jenny Woodcock
79 Tony Stone Images
82 Collections/Sandra Lousada
109 The Stock Market

ABOUT THE AUTHORS

Sheila Lavery is a freelance journalist who specialises in complementary medicine and mother and child health. She writes for a number of UK newspapers and magazines, including *The Express*, *Parents* magazine, *Family Life*, *Zest*, *Here's Health*, *Top Sante*, and *Essentials*. She is also the author of several books, including *The Healing Power of Sleep* and *Aromatherapy A Step-by-Step Guide*, and has contributed to the *Hamlyn Encyclopedia of Complementary Health*, *The Illustrated Encyclopedia of Healing Remedies* and the *Complete Family Guide to Alternative Medicine*. She is a member of the UK Guild of Health Writers.

Pippa Duncan has been a health writer for ten years, and writes on both conventional and complementary issues. She is the author of *A Parent's Guide to Complementary Healthcare for Children* and has contributed to a number of health-related books, including *The Illustrated Encyclopedia of Healing Remedies* and the *Complete Family Guide to Alternative Medicine*. Pippa is currently Features Editor on the UK magazine, *Parents*. She is a member of the UK Guild of Health Writers.

Pippa is married with two young sons – Jonah and Cameron.